S0-CAI-338

OMNIVM LVX CIVIVM

BOSTON
PUBLIC
LIBRARY

IN SMALL DOSES

Books for adults by Phyllis Naylor

Phyllis Naylor

IN SMALL DOSES

1979 NEW YORK *Atheneum*

Copyright © 1979 by Phyllis Naylor
All rights reserved
Library of Congress catalog card number 78-72978
ISBN 0-689-10962-8
Published simultaneously in Canada
by McClelland and Stewart Ltd.
Manufactured by American Book-Stratford Press,
Saddle Brook, New Jersey
Designed by Kathleen Carey
First Edition

TO HUSBANDS,
especially mine

CONTENTS

ONE

His and Hers

PASSING THE BUCK

After fifteen years of married life, one is bound to acquire a little wisdom, and Ralph and I could surely add a footnote or two to the marriage manuals.

It's uncanny the way the small problems that accumulate are never discussed in print. Where, for instance, have you read that the two most dangerous things a spouse can say are "Maybe your mother will do it," and "Go ask your father"?

It seemed so natural at first, so flattering. "Maybe your mother will do it," Ralph told Susan when he saw she'd put the doll's dress on backwards. "Go ask your father," I suggested when she asked where clouds came from. As the months went by, however, the flattery became an obvious pain-in-the-neck. I discovered I could get a ten-minute respite by sending our daughter to Ralph. And he quickly found that the easiest way to get out of an impossible task was to dump it in my lap. "Maybe your mother can do it," Ralph said when Susan presented him with her toy telephone which was hopelessly entangled with a Slinky.

When Jack came along, we grew more subtle.

"Has Daddy seen that new puzzle you got for your birthday?" I would suggest when Jack was underfoot in the kitchen, and Ralph would tell him, "Your mother is better at puzzles than I am." Sometimes Jack was shuttled back and forth like a tennis ball until one day he stopped halfway between the kitchen and living room and shouted, "Is someone going to play with me or not?"

When Peter was born, we declared a truce. Neither of us was to suggest, request, or otherwise infer that the other parent might be available for a choice piece of dirty work. Each of us was free to say no without being made to feel guilty.

There is nothing in the world, however, that can make you feel guilt quite as much as a small child with quivering lips announcing that the wheel of his wagon has rolled down the storm sewer. Still, we put up a united front.

"Will you get it for me?" Peter asks his father.

"No," says Ralph wearily.

"Will you, Mommy?"

"Not now," I answer, engrossed in a week's accumulation of newspapers.

"Maybe there will be a storm during the night and the wheel will wash away," Peter says tremulously. "Maybe an animal will carry it off or a robber will steal it." And when neither Ralph nor I budge from the comfort of our chairs, Peter opens his mouth and bellows, "What kind of parents are you guys, anyway?"

Answer: tired. "Wait till tomorrow, Peter, and we'll go to the hardware store and buy another."

A PRIVATE ENCOUNTER

Every year on our anniversary, Ralph sends me fourteen red roses. The deliveryman looks at me askance when I sign for "a dozen plus two," but it seems far too personal to explain that they stand for the fourteen reasons Ralph says he married me. (I can only remember eleven, anyway.) So I accept them gratefully and put them on the mantel, and the children stare like they're witnessing one of the tribal rituals they won't understand until they're older.

"I guess it means you're still in love," Susan said this time.

"I should hope to tell you," I replied. What did she think we were—a pair of antique clocks?

But Susan was serious. "How do you do it?" she insisted. "After all these years, you still like each other!"

"Work," I told her. "Constant attention to keeping alive whatever was attractive about us in the first place."

I didn't tell her, of course, that Ralph and I have a list of unwritten rules concerning our behavior, such as never criticizing each other in public, never contradicting each other's authority, never mentioning his premature balding or my premature graying (baldness and graying are always premature).

I'll admit that there have been some hassles we weren't too sure we could handle. Our sole surviving parent has a Solomon Complex (he believes he can solve any problem that might arise in our marriage simply by dividing everything in half, even though our last argument was over Peter). Consequently, we never confide anything in him. And the marriage manuals are either so outdated that they're useless or so advanced that they create more problems than they solve.

Last year, after a particularly emotional argument, we almost joined an encounter group. But when we heard that all the couples sat around nude and listened to a tape-recorded leader telling them to rub each other's back and listen to each other's stomach rumble and tell each other their most intimate secrets, we decided we'd been having private sessions all along and never knew it. So after the kids were in bed one night, we rubbed each other's back and listened to the other's stomach rumble and told each other our most intimate secrets, and finally we discovered we were talking over the big problem itself, and by two in the morning, we'd worked it out.

TRADE-OFF

Blame it on the full moon or the egg rolls or a hormonal imbalance, but two months ago Ralph and I had a ridiculous argument about which of us had to do the most crud around the house. We weren't talking about masculine versus feminine or which of us works the hardest or longest. We each simply felt that the jobs we had to do were the lousiest of the bunch and that somehow each of us was getting the raw end of the deal.

It is an unwritten law, you know, that when parents quarrel—raise their voices even one little decibel —the children will be listening. It is a simple solid fact that no matter how loudly you call them to dinner or ask them to clean their closets, they cannot hear you. But if one parent says anything to the other in a certain tone of voice, all noise will cease and the children, wherever they are stationed, will sit like zombies, waiting for the other shoe to drop.

Jack, however, decided this was one argument he

could settle himself.

"Why don't you trade the jobs you hate most?" he suggested. "Okay, Mom? That all right with you, Dad?"

Okay? It was a marvelous idea! Why hadn't we thought of it ourselves! Now was my chance to unload a real stinker on Ralph, something like cleaning the oven or sorting the socks or washing Peter's hair. I finally decided to trade the weekly scrubbing of the bathtub, and Ralph assigned me the weekly trip to the gas station.

"I won't even have to leave the house," Ralph chortled, "just take a rag and wash out the tub."

"It's a deal!" I cooed. "All I have to do is zip over to the gas station and ask the men to do the work."

The first week Ralph complained that the tub didn't look any cleaner after he'd washed it than before, and I explained that he had to use force. I complained that the gas had run down the side of the car and streaked it, and Ralph explained that I had to tell the men not to add any more after the pump clicks off.

The second week I screeched that there was white grit all over the bottom of the tub, and Ralph went upstairs to rinse it again. Then he discovered that all the valve caps on the tires were missing and told me I had to request the station attendants to put them back on each time they added air.

The third week Ralph did one side of the tub but forgot the other, and the station attendant forgot to wash the windshield, so I had to wash it myself.

The fourth week Ralph said he had a sore shoulder, and I said I'd be glad to do the tub for him that day if he'd take care of the car. That was a month ago. I've been scrubbing the tub ever since, and he's been dealing with the gas station, and if Jack will just mind his own business and not ask how the arrangement is working out, we'll never bring up the subject again.

OUR JUST REWARD

Some people may know it's spring when the flowers bloom, but I know it when the kids start wearing patched jeans, the last of winter's remnants before shorts set in, on Sundays.

The choir director knows it's spring when the Amens all end sharp instead of flat. The congregation knows it when they sing three new hymns in a row, all six verses yet! The school principal knows it when robins nest openly above the all-purpose room door. The teacher knows it when pussy willows appear on her desk. But husbands know spring by Form 1040 and the check stubs from last year.

This time, stalled somewhere between foreign corporations and the state gasoline tax, Ralph belatedly discovered that travel expenses for services rendered to charitable organizations are deductible at seven cents a mile.

"That means," he said, in growing comprehension, "that my duty as usher and yours as second soprano are good for seven times three miles times fifty-two weeks . . ."

"Plus travel to and from choir practice and board meetings and Cub Scouts and bake sales and P.T.A. suppers and lunchroom duty . . ." I added breathlessly.

"Not to mention the nights you spent repairing hymnals . . ."

"And the time you painted the school doors . . ."

"Or driving people to polling places . . ."

"Or the citizen's association . . ."

The dollars added up before my eyes. The IRS really cared. At long last there was justice and compensation for hard work. We had obviously spent a fortune in money, time, and effort for all mankind, and our reward was close at hand.

What about all the stockings I had snagged on the benches in the school cafeteria? What about the rabbits I'd contributed one Easter and the holly I gave at Christmas? What about the doctor's bill when I slipped at a spaghetti supper and sprained my leg? What about deducting all the paste and stencils and paper clips and . . . ?

"Twenty-eight dollars and seven cents," said Ralph.

The fortune disintegrated before our very eyes and we shrank to our proper proportions. We had sought compensation, when a "Well done, thou good and faithful servant" should have sufficed.

ON QUESTIONS AND CURIOSITY

I had always imagined that children would ask profound questions when we were sitting around the fire or walking along the beach or listening to a Haydn quartet. That was before I knew anything about children.

Last week, during a heated discussion of our electric bill and what we could do to save energy, Peter asked what apples were made of. I stopped thinking about amps and volts and was trying to concentrate on nutrients, when Ralph said simply,

"Skin, seeds, and pulp."

"Oh," said Peter.

Now why couldn't I have thought of that?

When Susan was three, she did not ask me where

babies came from in the privacy of our living room. She waited until we were on a crowded elevator and then, when it stopped to pick up a very pregnant woman, she bellowed, "How did that baby get inside her, Mommy?" (I told her I'd tell her as soon as we got back to the car, and I did.)

Friday was another one of those days. Peter had been home from school for one hour, stuffing his face with crackers, but waited until the Sears van drove up with my new washer to ask what was on his mind:

"If you had married someone else, would I still be me?"

"Wait a minute, Peter," I said, and I told the deliverymen if they went around to the den door, they'd have an easier time of it. Then I went downstairs to unlock the back door.

"No, you wouldn't, Peter," I said. "If you had a different father, you'd be a different person."

I opened the door and watched while the men tried to wedge the washer between my desk and the file cabinets.

"But half of him would still be me," Peter insisted.

"Listen, lady, this isn't going to work," one of the deliverymen said. "We've got to take it around front, go up your steps, and then come down the stairs from inside."

"Okay," I said, and hurried back up to clear a path through the living room.

"Well, I guess that's right," I told Peter, "half of

you would still be you, but it would be all mixed up with a different half."

I held the door open for the deliverymen and signed a form which said they weren't responsible if they ruined my rug.

"Would the half that was really me know that the other half was somebody else?" Peter insisted. The deliverymen looked at him warily.

"Down there," I said, directing them to the basement.

"Or would the new half of me be the real half and know that the old half was different?" Peter went on. "What if the new half was a girl half? Would I still be Peter? Or would the old half...?"

At that moment Ralph called and wanted me to look up a figure on our income tax form.

"Just a minute, dear," I said. "Meanwhile, Peter has a question he wants to ask..."

I gave the phone to Peter with the knowledge that he would keep Ralph occupied until I could find the information he wanted, or the washing machine was installed, or I had my wits about me once more, whichever came first.

THE SEGMENTED SELF

I have never been impressed with unisex anything, be it clothing or haircuts. I am particularly annoyed with those who claim that men and women think the same way, because anyone married for fifteen years knows it just isn't true. Whether by heredity or environment, males and females have different compartments in their brains for storing facts and figures, and what one sex labels "Of Prime Importance," better known as OPI, the other scarcely bothers about from one month to the next.

I am physically incapable, for example, of remembering to get my car greased and the oil changed every six months. I am quite able to remember which brand of underwear belongs to Peter and which to Jack, what clothes must be dry-cleaned, or how long it has been since Susan washed her hair, but I have never succeeded in remembering to change the furnace filter.

Ralph, on the other hand, has no difficulty whatsoever in remembering the expiration dates on all our assorted warranties or sending the mortgage payments in on time. But if I call him at work and ask him to pick up Peter at a friend's house or stop at the store for a loaf of bread, he rarely fails to arrive home empty-handed.

After a while, I suppose, our brains, like our lives, get segmented into sections, and Peter is automatically placed in the women's department along with a loaf of bread as far as Ralph is concerned. I, in turn, give the mortgage payments no more attention than I give the underside of the car. Never mind that in other families where the husband stays home with the children, the OPI's are reversed. Married people, unlike their single counterparts, always divide up the work, and their brains are never the same again.

It wouldn't hurt, I know, to assign the checkbook balancing to me for six months and the cooking to Ralph. It would give each of us a taste of the other's domain and make us sympathetic to the other's problems. But every time we consider it, we remember how I once wrote a check for the entire balance of our account, and how one night Ralph put a chicken still covered with plastic wrap in the oven. And because we would rather forget, we continue our segmented lives, grateful we have each other.

EXTENSIONS OF OURSELVES

I have heard it said that there is a close relationship between a man and his car, and that a wife should be just as careful about criticizing one as the other. A car, psychiatrists say, is an extension of man's self, and this must explain Ralph's anxiety if the Plymouth coughs, wheezes, or snorts. It explains why he lifts the hood and listens hopefully for signs of life, why he carries his own special oil in the trunk, and why he absolutely refuses to drive it anywhere if it has a dent.

Herein lies the vast difference between the psychology of men and women. I would drive a car with three wheels and missing fenders if I could be sure it would get me where I was going. I care not whether it is big or little, clean or dirty, new or old. If it starts when I turn the key, that's all I require of it.

If I have extensions of self, it's more likely to be the children. Though I steadfastly reject the idea that children are put on this earth to glorify their mother who sitteth at home, deep down in my heart of hearts

I want them to represent me well.

It appalls me, for instance, if Jack and Peter go off to school with dirty ears, and I must be the only mother on the block who waves a Q-tip as they leave, calling them back.

"Nobody cares, Mom!" Jack protests. "None of the other guys go around looking in my ears!"

"Your teacher does."

"She doesn't have time!" Jack argues, and he's probably right.

But what *would* she think if she looked in his ears and found them yucky? That I'm a negligent mother? That we are a family of slatterns? That, heaven forbid, my own ears are dirty?

"She'd probably just think I got up late and didn't have a chance to wash," Jack said.

I wonder, sometimes, if I tend to look at my family as possessions, existing for my benefit. There are days when Ralph must feel like a chauffeur, driving us about on vacations; when the children must feel they are merely errand boys or housemaids; when all of them must feel I enjoy them most when *I* want them, forgetting that they in turn need me.

It helps to remember that while Susan, Jack, and Peter exist because of me, they do not exist for me. Ralph was here before I was born and would have made it whether I had come along or not. And while the Good Book mentions clean hands and a pure heart, it says nothing whatsoever about ears.

A MUTUAL UNDERSTANDING

My grandmother used to say that it is not the big things that cause stress in a marriage, it's the little things. I never believed her until now. Looking back, I can report that there are indeed small details of living that could have been blown up out of all proportion if we'd let them.

Let me give you an example: I would never have thought that a simple bowl of oatmeal could come between us. Ralph has a particular fondness for the stuff and, as his dutiful wife, I have made the making of oatmeal an art: the right amount of water, the appropriate pinch of salt, the added raisins, and the proper "curing." Consequently, when Ralph sits down to breakfast, I have timed the dish so that it appears instantly before him, a big rich mound of gray matter, speckled with raisins, which—if I had my way—would be gently surrounded with a small amount of cream, sprinkled with brown sugar, and eaten instantly.

I never get my way. Without even looking at the

dish, Ralph reaches for the skim milk and completely inundates the oatmeal with this watery-blue fluid. And then, while he reads the front page and lingers over his orange juice, he allows my culinary masterpiece to congeal.

I have tried giving it to him *after* he drinks his juice. Same problem. He reads the editorial page before he touches it. I have tried bribing and cajoling with no success. Ralph's position, perfectly justified, is that it is *his* oatmeal, going into *his* stomach, to be enjoyed as *he* sees fit. So why can't I accept it? What possible difference does it make to me, except that I imagine I can hear the oatmeal hissing in protest as it drowns bit by bit in the skim milk?

Ralph, of course, puts up with a lot from me. There is no other woman in Bethesda, my family tells me, who starts so many sentences and finishes so few of them. I guess I feel that when they obviously know what I'm going to say next, there's no earthly reason to say it. But if Ralph can stand to hear me remark at the breakfast table each morning, "It's going to be a sunny day, so I guess you won't need . . ." without finishing it, then I can look across at his coagulated oatmeal with equanimity.

THE GET-AWAY PLAN

Yes, I know exactly how it got started: with the births of Susan, Jack, and Peter, to be precise. It used to be that Ralph and I could laze away Saturday mornings in bed if we liked, or, for that matter, the afternoons as well. We could eat when and what we liked, take off for the ocean on a moment's notice, come home at any hour of the night, and buy concert tickets without the constant worry that somebody would be throwing up that night.

Then the kids arrived, one at a time to be sure, and a wee voice with the command of a bugle had us floundering out of bed at five in the morning. We found our shopping carts invaded with jars of strained beets and bananas, and there was no such thing as going off to the ocean on a moment's notice. It took an hour just to pack the playpen, the crib, the potty, and all the other equipment essential to a toddler in training pants.

Of course, we still managed to get out occasionally, having first (1) hired a sitter two weeks in advance; (2) made dinner for both sitter and sittee; (3)

cleaned the house in case the sitter's mother dropped by; (4) left a list of instructions by the telephone in case one of the kids tried to swallow a button; (5) promised said sitter, who always had to be home a half-hour before the concert was over, that we would miss the last movement of Beethoven's Fifth and come dashing back to have her home by eleven.

Even now, with the children older, going out for the evening still means rushing through dinner, settling quarrels to make sure there is no cause for violence while we're gone, rehashing the old argument about who's in charge, and finally dashing downtown. Then one day we discovered we weren't enjoying it much.

We began to talk about a sixth-month sabbatical from the children when we would go to Polynesia and send the kids to boarding school or, better yet, send *them* to Polynesia so we could stay blissfully at home.

We worked out a compromise. Four times a year, once each season, both Ralph and I take an entire day (always a day when the kids are in school) and evening off from work. We send them off with lunch money, instructions about dinner, and phone numbers —all of which have been worked out in advance. Then, with fourteen hours or so before us, we leisurely dress and have breakfast. We wander through art galleries, go to lunch, attend a matinée, browse through a bookstore, stroll through a park, have a long dinner hour in a favorite spot, drive along the

Potomac, and finally, when we're good and ready, go home. No rush, no hurry—a long, long day to fill in as we like. This is what honeymoons are made of.

The children tolerate these weird quarterly flights. They call them our "get-away kicks." They can call them whatever they like; after one of those seasonal sojourns, we feel rested, relaxed, and able to endure another three months of frenzied living.

All I ask, when these same children are grown and married and feel the same need for flight, is that they make their own arrangements and not leave their kids with us.

LOVE AND MARRIAGE

It was over in thirty seconds or less. I reminded Ralph of a letter he had to write, and his reply indicated that he was old enough to remember such things by himself. That was all. After the door closed, I silently promised to quit treating him like one of the children, and he probably resolved to keep up with his correspondence. We both knew, from a kind of security one gets after being married for so long, that we would be glad to see each other again at the end of the day.

But the kids, never having been married at all, come unglued over flashes of anger between us. Somehow, a sarcastic voice or a sullen glare triggers an alarm at the base of the brain, and a child will hang around for reassurance that there is still love to spare.

On this particular morning, the alarm rang in Jack. The moment Ralph had left, Jack turned to me and said, "Mom, do you think you would have been happier if you'd married somebody else?"

This ten-year-old philosopher, see, wants an answer in twenty-five seconds to a question that some people ponder their whole lifetime.

"Probably so," I said, basing my answer on statistics. "When you consider that the number of men I dated were only a fraction of the men in my town and scarcely a speck of the men in the world, it is very probable that there are many men who might have suited me better."

There were gasps from Susan and Peter across the table. It wasn't fair, really, ripping away their security blankets so early in the morning. Susan's lips trembled. "Mo—ther!" she said. "I thought you and Daddy were happy!"

"But we are!" I explained. "That's what love is all about, my dear. We only meet a handful of people in our lives, and we choose among them. When you marry, it's never the best man in the whole wide world, but simply one about whom you care very much. You joyfully make the decision to share your life with him, faults included, and that's sort of nice, when you think about it."

I don't know if I got through to them or not. Susan would rather believe that couples are matched in heaven. But when one thinks of the number of people who are married after one week in Las Vegas, or who recite their vows while skydiving over a field in Kansas or sitting together on the back of a motorcycle, I rather think that heaven, too, merely hopes for the best.

SWAP

Though happily married, I must admit to the occasional desire to swap: not spouses, only their habits.

It could be arranged on a perfectly regulated basis. I would swap one of Ralph's annoying mannerisms for one of those of a neighbor, provided the husbands cooperated, of course. It would mean that for one week I would no longer have to watch Ralph drown his hot oatmeal in a deluge of cold skim milk. Instead, I would listen to him say, "Is your garbage ready to go out?" which for some reason drives the woman across the street absolutely bananas.

I don't know. I think I could take that very well, but I wonder. If I heard it every day for a week . . . a month . . . a year . . . fifteen years?

Perhaps, for one week, I could trade off Ralph's habit of draping his jogging socks over his shoe rack in exchange for a neighbor's habit of coughing each morning before he opens his car door. I would even take the way the man on the corner inspects his lawn on his hands and knees every Saturday if I could exchange the way Ralph lets mail accumulate on his reading stand.

Maybe we ought to try it. Maybe I ought to promise Ralph that he could trade off some habits of mine in the bargain. But then again . . .

I'm sort of used to those little mannerisms of mine. They're a part of me—like a leg or an arm. It would be absolutely wrenching to give them up.

Let's not rush into anything, now. What's oatmeal, after all? What are dangling socks? What is a reading stand piled high with unanswered mail as long as I can continue to overcook the spaghetti and use up all the hot water before Ralph has had his bath?

THE INDISPENSABLE

Everyone wants to believe he is indispensable— that the office or the home or the team or the guild would collapse if he weren't holding it up. I'm no exception. It's simply that I *know* the family would collapse without me, that's all, and if you doubt it, consider just one wee fact: I'm the only one who knows where the winter clothes are stored.

Who else knows that the washing machine has to go one and a half cycles before the clothes are properly rinsed, or that the nutmeg is in the bottle marked paprika? Who else knows that the third tile from the left above the tub is being held in place with double-stick tape, or that the chicken in the freezer ought to be used before the pork roast?

If the proper rearing of children means getting them weaned fast, I'd better get a move on, because they'd starve if something happened to me. No, not starve. They would survive on pizza, which Jack knows how to order by phone; angel food cake, which Susan knows how to make from a mix; peanut butter and crackers, which Peter know how to put together; and an unlimited quantity of hard-boiled eggs and canned soup, which are Ralph's only culinary accomplishments.

When I had my first baby, it was decided that we would not ask my mother to come because Ralph could take care of everything. An hour after I got home from the hospital I was in the kitchen making dinner, having found that easier than an oral dissertation on where the pans were stored, how to use the oven, and the difference between braise, broil, and simmer gently.

I am not belittling Ralph. Cooking comes easy for one who has done it three times a day for fifteen years. Yet I would be the first to admit that if anything went wrong with the car while I was driving, I would not only be unable to set up the jack, but could not even raise the hood. My ignorance knows no bounds.

When you come right down to it, there is something that is irreplaceable in us all. Susan plays the piano in a style quite her own; Jack has an inimitable way of telling a story; six-year-old Peter has a charm about him I could never duplicate if I had fifteen more children; and Ralph's sense of humor and his perspective have seen me through more difficulties than I care to admit. As for me, I could always *tell* somebody where I keep the winter clothes and where I hide the nutmeg, but I like to know I'm needed.

OLD LOVES

A year ago I gave Ralph a new pair of slippers for Christmas. They weren't elegant or unusual or rakish, even. Just an ordinary pair of slippers exactly like the ones he'd been wearing for the last five years, which were ripped at the back seam and frayed on the inside.

He thanked me, of course, but confided later that there was really nothing wrong with his old slippers that a needle and thread wouldn't fix, and as for the insides, well, nobody ever saw them.

I took the biggest needle and the strongest thread I could find and went to work, feeling guilty about the nine dollars I had spent for slippers he didn't need. The thread broke, the leather split, and when the needle broke as well, I took the slippers to a shoe repair shop where I was told that the cost of sewing the back seams alone would be seven dollars.

Outraged, indignant—triumphant, even—I returned home and told Ralph that there was no way in the world his old slippers could be salvaged. Nevertheless, he had them on again that night and the night after that, the new slippers reposing on the top shelf of his closet.

By this Christmas his old slippers were in such a state that not only were the heels split and the linings frayed, but the soles were coming loose at the toes.

"Helps ventilate the feet," Ralph remarked to no one in particular.

Feeling sure that he had forgotten the new slippers, I got them down, wrapped them again, and put them under the tree. I was right. He'd forgotten. But he gazed tenderly down at those leather remnants over his socks and said, "Still six months' wear left in the old ones."

What is it about husbands? Is a comfortable pair of old slippers a teddy-bear substitute, do you think? Is it a concern for waste and thrift? Is it a grudge against the United Shoe-Workers Union or whatever? Is it to put me to shame for owning three pair of shoes to every one of his?

No matter. He fell down the stairs yesterday. It wasn't a bad fall—just a slip, really—but somehow the flapping sole of one slipper got caught on the torn heel of the other, Ralph's feet crossed, and the next thing we knew he was sliding down the stairs like a giant tree.

We stared in silence and respect as he picked himself up and realigned his branches. We expected him to deposit his slippers in the waste basket. We expected him to say he had seen the light. Instead, he inspected each slipper to make sure it still had a sole and put them back on his feet.

I haven't the faintest idea how the story will end, and I'm wondering what it will take to get rid of his old college sweater.

IN SMALL DOSES

I could cope with my family very well if I could only take them by appointment. It's not the long list of chores that staggers me, but the fact that no matter what I set out to do, I am interrupted three or four times before it's done.

Breakfast? Put three eggs on to fry and instantly there is a plaintive "Mom!" from upstairs.

"What is it, Peter?"

"Come here."

"Just tell me. I'm making breakfast."

"I can't wear these pants. They're too tight."

"Wear your brown ones then."

"I can't find them."

"Look on the left side of your closet."

"I did!"

With eggs sputtering menacingly, I rush upstairs, whisk out the trousers, and rush back down just as the phone rings. It's Ralph.

"I left a patient folder on my desk, and I've got to cancel his session," he explains. "Would you look on the cover page and give me his phone number?"

I heard the toast pop.

"Could I call you back after I get the kids' breakfast?"

"I have to reach him before nine-thirty."

"Okay, I'll do it now."

I get the number for Ralph, hang up, and try to butter cold toast. Susan doesn't want a fried egg. She says she's told me a thousand times to make hers scrambled, and she's right. I start to cook another.

"Mom, did I tell you I have to have a check for our field trip?" Jack says, sliding in his chair. He jars the table and spills the orange juice. I set him to work cleaning it up and go get the checkbook.

The phone rings again.

"Honey," comes Ralph's maddeningly calm voice, "that number's been disconnected. Look on the bottom of the cover page and see if I didn't scribble his new number in pencil."

There is the smell of burning egg from the kitchen, and I rescue Susan's breakfast too late. She says the smell makes her sick, and if she tried to eat anything now, she'd throw up. Peter is toasting another slice of bread but has buttered it before putting it in the toaster. I pull out the plug, rush to the den to get a second number and give it to Ralph.

"Thanks a million," he says. "Incidentally, did

you get to the editorial page yet? There's a good column by Jack Anderson . . ."

That's the difference, you see. Ralph gets all his problems in small doses, by appointment. I get mine all at once, and usually at breakfast.

TWO

Ours

THE PATIENCE GAP

I thought I knew all about babies before I had any of my own. Really. I had child psychology courses in college, natural childbirth courses, Red Cross baby-care courses, and a stint of psychotherapy for parents-to-be. I knew that children would mean hours of hard work and sacrifice, and I was prepared. Diapers? Teething? Bring them on, said I. Motherhood, here I come.

Looking back, I see three magnificent misconceptions. The first was that babies, like dolls, lie quietly on their backs and coo while they are being diapered and dressed. I simply was not prepared for the fact that arms and legs move constantly, heads jerk and bodies twist. I was astounded by the vigor with which a three-month old can kick. The reason you don't see more little kids in frilly dresses or sailor suits is that the parents are exhausted after the diaper and rubber pants.

Second, I had visions of my toddler sitting happily in his playpen surrounded by blocks and rubber ducks. I did not know that children develop an allergy to the playpen within minutes of being in it, or that even when you let them out they crawl between your feet and whine piteously to be picked up.

Third, I thought that if you had studied child psychology, you would automatically handle correctly every situation that came along. I did not realize that it is one thing to *know* what to say, and another to say it. I knew what to say when Susan spilled fingerpaint on our bedspread. I knew what to say when Jack climbed up a tree and wouldn't come down. I knew what to say when Peter took off all his clothes and dropped them out the car window. But I didn't know there would be times when I would *want* to embarrass or shame or frighten my children; when I seemed, for a moment, to *want* them to feel stupid. I had to confront the monster in me before I realized how far I still had to go to be mature.

"What do you want for your birthday, Mommy?" Peter asked yesterday.

Patience, I thought, as I sat him on my knee. *Self-control. Empathy.* But we talked instead of eggbeaters and ballpoint pens, and he ran happily off to count his pennies.

CAREERS AND KIDS

If you asked me what I would like my children to become, I would probably say what most parents say, "Whatever makes them happy." We don't exactly mean it, of course. What we want to say is "something safe and socially acceptable, equal to our own occupational status or better." But we don't say that. We tell our kids to develop their own potential and we'll love them regardless.

What Susan, Jack, and Peter will become is anyone's guess. Susan has gone through the airline stewardess bit, and lately has been talking about being either a veterinarian or a sculptress. Jack toys with the idea of being a reporter or an anthropologist or possibly even a poet. Now who could argue with any of these? But Peter is a different story.

The first thing Peter ever expressed an interest in being was a garbage man. He watched bug-eyed as big-muscled men leaped off monstrous trucks, lifted the huge cans, and then tossed them twenty feet before rolling off again in a cloud of dust. What a life!

This too shall pass, I told myself. And it did. It was replaced by a mad desire to be a garage mechanic. Well, I told myself, the world needs mechanics as well as poets. But now Peter has changed his mind again. Now he knows what he was made to be: a rock star.

I would rather my child had lice. An announcement like this, to a mother who was raised on Bach and Beethoven, can destroy her very soul. Is this child mine, I wondered, staring at his cherubic little face. Where did I go wrong? What on earth would turn his fancies to an Alice Cooper rather than an Albert Schweitzer or someone like that?

Ralph, however, is not disturbed in the least. He doesn't believe that Peter will grow up to be a rock star any more than he believes that Peter will grow wings.

"He's only six," he tells me. "Think what you wanted to be when you were that age."

Do I have to? A movie actress, of course—one of those sinuous things in a leopard skin who was always drifting along on a raft with Tarzan. Then in a complete about-face, I was going to be a missionary to China. That lasted a year and a half before I considered being a tap dancer, an opera singer, and a teacher, in that order.

The movie industry and the Metropolitan Opera never knew what they were missing. I don't know what effect I'd have had upon China or an elementary classroom, but I guess Providence decided I ought to stay home and write. Who knows what will be decided for Peter?

THE AGING PROCESS

The kids are growing up, and I don't like it. I used to think that once they could entertain themselves on a rainy day, I would have it made. I used to think that once they were toilet-trained and could tie their own shoelaces, life would be nirvana. Oh brother, was I wrong!

The thing about kids eight or under is that you can, for the most part, count on them. You know where they are, you know they will put on the shirts you laid out for them, and you know you will have them in bed before ten o'clock. Even if you *know* that they will get sick the day you leave on vacation or embarrass you in front of company, at least you know and can take it into account.

We don't even have a teenager yet and already life has become uncertain. Ralph and I used to be able to plan an evening out when we felt like it, because Susan was always available as a sitter. Now Susan has plans of her own.

When the children's heads came no higher than

our elbows, the air space from waist to eye level belonged to Ralph and myself, and we could discuss all manner of private things in their presence just by mouthing the words to each other or talking right over their heads.

But no more.

"What did you say happened to Mrs. Kenibark?" Susan will say at the first hint of gossip.

"What did you just say to Daddy?" Peter will ask as he notices a whispered exchange.

"Can I read Grandpa's letter?" Jack will ask, not content with the line or two I had singled out for his benefit.

There are all sorts of worries now that I didn't have before. When the children were little, they always rode with me. Now when Jack or Susan is invited to spend a weekend in the country with a friend, how do I investigate the family diplomatically? How long can I go on taking case histories of all those whom my children encounter? When they are in a car with an unknown driver, the umbilical cord will stretch just so far.

Last night, when I playfully complained that the children were growing up too fast, Peter said, "So what do you want me to do, Mommy—grow backwards?"

It's a thought. What if, when your child reached that impossible age (to be determined by the parents), he began to regress until he was a lovable little six-month-old baby again who slept all day with his panda? Would I exchange the anxiety I feel when Susan's out on the highway at night for a load of dirty diapers and evening colic? I don't know. Give me a week or two to think it over.

OF BANAL BANTER

Isn't there some religion where you aren't supposed to talk at the table? Aren't there countries where people believe that if you open your mouth at mealtime for anything but food, demons will fly in and infest the soul?

I want to go there. I want a table where the only communication allowed is "Pass the salt" or "No, thanks." But until Jack and Peter reach the age of civility, whatever that is, I'm not going to get it, of this I'm sure.

If there were a prize for banality at mealtime, our boys would win it hands down. Even Susan has been heard to bemoan the lack of intelligent conversation at dinner. If the boys aren't arguing over whose roll is the biggest or who is kicking whom under the table, they invent a game whose singular goal, it seems, is to drive us all mad. It continues nonstop through soup and salad and entrée and dessert, and because one always takes over when the other stops for breath, it is virtually impossible to change the subject.

Take last night. Peter declared that if all the things in the world that were spelled with five letters belonged to him, he would be king of the universe.

"What do you mean?" Ralph asked. That was our first mistake. We should have instantly agreed and filled him up with mashed potatoes.

"Paper," said Peter, as though that explained it. "Think of all the stuff that's made out of paper!"

Jack jumped in with both feet. "If *I* owned everything that was spelled with *four* letters, *I'd* be king," he contested. "What about sand? Every grain of sand counts. I'm king!"

"Grass!" declared Peter hotly. "I get all the blades of grass."

"I get all the rain—every single drop!"

"Water!"

"You can't have it! I already said rain!"

If we'd had our wits about us, we would have told the boys they were both winners. We would have said the world contained so many marvelous things that we could not possibly count them all. Instead, we silently finished our green beans, studied the meat loaf, and tried without success to remember the melody of Brahm's Third.

KEEPING TAB

They say that as we get older, our memories fail us, and we can't remember from one moment to the next where we put our glasses. However bad mine might be, the kids' memories are even worse.

I'm not talking about their inability to remember relatives' middle names. I'm not even talking about their relapse when it comes to daily chores or the multiplication tables. I just want to know why it is that they can't remember to close the door when the air conditioner is on and to leave it open when it's not.

In fact, they don't even have to think about air conditioning.

"If the door was closed when you came in, close it again after you," I tell them. "If it was open, leave it open."

It doesn't work. Susan, Jack, and Peter are congenitally incapable of this simple manual feat. If the day is warm and breezy and the doors are wide open, Peter will invariably stop and shut the door firmly when he comes inside. If it is 92 degrees and the air conditioning has been on for a week, Jack will come bursting in, hot and thirsty, and leave the door wide open. Susan, however, is at least aware of the problem. She can't remember if the door was open or closed, it's true, but at least she'll stand in the doorway and screech, "Do you want the door open or shut, Mom?"

Come to think of it, this memory thing is pretty selective. Do they ever for a moment forget that once when they asked us to take them on the world's fastest roller coaster we said, "Maybe"? Do they ever forget that when they asked if they could have a ten-speed bike with a banana seat, we replied, "We'll see"?

They never forget. They know the year, the month, the day, and the hour one socked the other, so when we bawl them out for fighting, they can claim they are just getting even and back it up with facts. They'll make good voters, these kids. When their candidate is elected, they'll never let him forget his campaign promises. Never. Even unto the fourth generation.

A JOKING MATTER

When Peter was only four, his favorite pastime for a while was asking adults a riddle: "How do you keep a bull from charging?" and when they answered with the traditional "I don't know," Peter would answer, "Take away his credit card," and then laugh uproariously. Finally, however, after he had tried it on a waitress at a restaurant, he turned to me and asked, "What's a credit card?"

Jokes, of course, are impossible to keep secret. Start off a good joke in a night club in San Francisco and it will be repeated in a nursery school in Boston a month later. As jaded parents of three, Ralph and I keep telling ourselves that "now we've heard everything," but then a new joke comes along and we discover we haven't.

Last night at the dinner table, for example, with Gramps as guest, I hardly blinked an eye when Jack said, "Hey, Gramps, what's white and crawls up your leg?"

"I don't know, son," said Gramps. "What?"

"Uncle Ben's perverted rice!" Jack chortled, and

45]

Gramps choked on his chicken soup.

Not to be outdone, however, Susan asked if we'd heard the latest "Mommy" joke:

"Mommy, Mommy! I don't want to go to England!"

"Shut up, and keep swimming."

Gramps was still thinking that over when Jack came up with another:

"Mommy, Mommy! Daddy has a wound!"

"Quit complaining, and eat around it."

Ralph and I called an instant halt to jokes at that point, but later in the kitchen I thought about it. I suppose in any society, kids are thrust into adult concerns and situations long before they're ready for them. But intimations of perversion? Shades of sadism? Cannibalism, even? Were they ready for that? I heard Jack, who is only ten, go by the kitchen door singing, "My yesterdays are all gone by," and a few minutes after that, Peter was singing, ". . . makin' love in my Chevy van, and that's all right with me."

If they're thinking and talking and singing like this now, I wondered, what will they be doing when they're twenty? Then I remembered the bull and the credit card, and knew that Jack has plenty of tomorrows coming his way, regardless of what happened to his yesterdays. As for Chevy vans, I asked Peter later what he would do in a van if he had one, and he said, "Eat potato chips and stuff." Adulthood's still a long way off.

THE SALOME SYNDROME

It's a good thing I have only one daughter and two sons. If I'd had two twelve-going-on-thirteen-year-old daughters, I'd be weak in the knees and living on Miltown. If all three had been daughters, I'd be spending every other month in a sanitarium.

At some certain age, in the life of every girl, the Salome Syndrome sneaks in, evidenced by the paranoia that every male, young or old, healthy or otherwise, is looking at her. Consequently, everything about her must be perfect.

"Mo—ther!" Susan shrieks. It is always a shriek. One rushes headlong upstairs, expecting to find a body at the very least, only to see a young girl staring in horror at the mirror.

"It's only you," I answer her. You never know when twelve-year-olds are going to develop amnesia.

"Look!" she shrieks again, pointing to her waist-line, and before I have a chance to advise or console or suggest, she flings herself toward the bathroom, howling that she is going to eat nothing but celery until the Fourth of July.

That wouldn't be half bad, I decide, when I see what comes next. Jogging, Susan decides, is the only way to slim down, and the only time she can do it without being seen is six o'clock in the morning. If she gets ready for school first, however, she'll just have to shower all over again, but if she goes directly from her bed to the sidewalk and meets anyone she knows, she'll absolutely die. No matter that the only person out at that hour is the milkman, and he is one year short of retirement.

In the event she *should* be seen unwashed, uncombed, and puffing, however, Susan hits upon the idea of wearing a hooded raincoat which comes down so far over her face that only her bottom lip shows. The sleeves hang down below her fingertips and only her ankles protrude from underneath. Every morning at 6:01, this rubberized apparition moves silently out the door. Fifteen minutes later, it reenters the kitchen, sheds its rubber skin, and rushes back upstairs to weigh in.

Sometime this twelve-year-old daughter of mine is going to trip on the hem of her raincoat and go sprawling, instantly drawing a crowd. She will either have to pick herself up and swallow her pride, or play dead in her rubberized paraphernalia and await identification at the hospital. In any case, I'll know it is Susan the moment I enter the emergency room and hear her first shriek.

THE DISCIPLINE DILEMMA

I learned long ago never to complain to a neighbor about something his child had done because as soon as I did, my own would do something worse. And it's hard enough to discipline our own kids without taking on the block as well.

I'm not against physical punishment, but I soon discovered that a hard whack on the bottom is equally hard on the hand, and despite the proverb about sparing the rod and spoiling the child, belts and hair brushes as instruments of torture never appealed to me much.

My father says that all I have to do is make the punishment fit the crime. When the children scribble on the walls, make them wash it off. When they break a window, make them pay for it out of their allowance. But what is appropriate punishment for a six-year-old who takes the goldfish out of the bowl and sprays them with the garden hose? What punishment is relevant for a ten-year-old who tells a neighbor everything you ever said about her? And if a twelve-going-on-thirteen-year-old girl turns one of her rings around and convinces her friends she is secretly married, do you make her do all the housework for a week to give her a taste of married life? If a boy dyes his skin with green ink, do you send him to school looking like Dracula, or do you simply charge him for the ink?

There are those, of course, who advocate no punishment at all. There are those who say that good behavior should be rewarded and bad behavior ignored. I can certainly understand how it might be very effective to ignore a child when he rudely demands a piece of cake. But if, on receiving no response, he reaches over and takes his little brother's, do you just sit there and look mournful? Do you tell him politely that his brother is displeased? Or do you wheel around and whallop him hard on the bottom?

The problem with books on discipline is that they never discuss the situations that come up at our house. I am perfectly capable of handling a child who spends all his allowance on Popsicles and hasn't any left to buy the model plane he's been wanting. But try as I might, I've never found a single suggestion regarding what a parent should do when a child cuts off the legs of his best trousers so his knees will be cool.

A WISP OF DOUBT

One of the reasons we don't have pets is because I can't understand them. If a goldfish rolls over on his side, I don't know what he's trying to tell me. If a dog merely stares sad-eyed at his supper, is he bored? In pain? Or sick to death of dry rations?

I can't even understand my own children at times, who have perfectly acceptable vocal chords. I understand the words, but I'm confused as to the meaning. Last month, for example, because Peter's sneakers were in such awful shape, I took him to buy another pair. It was a time convenient for me but not at all for Peter, who was building a battleship out of boxes in our basement. Consequently, he said yes to the first pair he tried on, eager to get home again.

Two days later he said that the sneakers hurt and he could run faster in his old ones. The day after that he said maybe there was something wrong down around the toes, and anyway, none of the other guys had green sneakers. The third day he said the new sneakers hurt more than ever and that Bobby Miller had told him he looked like a freak in them.

51]

The shoes looked fine to me. The salesman had assured me they fit him. And so I told Peter in no uncertain terms that these were his shoes for the next six months, that he had okayed them at the store, and he might as well make up his mind to wear them.

Then the drama began. Every morning Peter went off to school limping. Every afternoon he kicked them off as soon as he got home, screaming that he could barely walk. What's a parent to do? Would he be crippled for life just for the sake of eleven dollars and ninety-eight cents? Was it fair to insist that the pain was psychological when only Peter could possibly know?

I wish I could say that we resolved it intelligently. What happened was that one shoe somehow got in the garbage can and was carried off by the trash men, thereby making the other obsolete. Anybody who believes that the sneakers really hurt Peter's feet will probably believe that the disappearance of the shoe was accidental. As for me, I marched Peter off to the store a second time and left him there alone for thirty minutes to ponder his choice. I told him that when I came back, he was to have chosen a pair of new sneakers for better or worse, in sickness and in health, till death did them part—death or a larger shoe size, whichever came first.

LABOR DAY

It's as traditional as the return of the swallows to Capistrano. The day the children go back to school, I clean out their rooms. It's a job that has to be done in solitude. If the kids were around, they would salvage everything I threw out.

"Just don't give away my old hockey shirt," Jack yells on his way out the door.

"Don't throw out my ant farm!" Peter cautions. "There were two ants left, but I think they ate each other up."

"Don't read any of the letters in my drawer!" Susan bellows.

Thus restricted, I enter their rooms with a monstrous wastebasket and begin.

Why is it always worse than I imagine? Why have I failed to notice that accumulating pile of school papers and T-shirts in the back of the closet? How long has the top desk drawer been crammed so full it can't be opened, and why on earth does Susan need forty-seven rollers for one head of hair?

The day I found a week-old hamburger in Peter's toy chest was surpassed only by the time I reached far back in Jack's desk and pulled out the skeletal remains of a frog from science class. This time, however, the only surprise was a green silk box beneath Susan's pillow. I decided not to open it.

"Hey, Mom, it looks great!" Susan said that afternoon, and then her eyes fell on the green box. "Oh, you found it, huh?"

"Yes, but I didn't open it."

"Oh, it's okay. It's only my Tommy-Maloney-Faith-Hope-Charity-box, that's all."

"Your what?"

"Tommy-Maloney-Faith-Hope-Charity-box," Susan repeated. "Look, I'll show you."

I decided I'd better sit down. Susan opened the lid and pulled out a sixty-nine-cent ring. "This is the ring Tommy gave me when he broke up with Kay Hartley. This is my faith that he means it when he says he likes me better than her." She dipped down into the box again and pulled out a rabbit's foot. "This is my hope that I'll be lucky in love, and Tommy will forget all about Kay." Then she picked up a photo of a somewhat chubby girl with pigeon-toed feet. "And this is a picture of Kay Hartley," Susan said. "This is charity, because if Tommy ever does go back to Kay, I'll just look at this photograph and feel sorry for him, and then I won't get mad about it."

She closed the box and left the room, and I wondered if the Apostle Paul knew just how far his influence would extend when he wrote that letter to the Corinthians.

[54

S. Y. K. DAY

Jack was in a rotten mood when school started this year. Nothing was right. He'd wanted a *Star Wars* lunch box and the only thing left was a *Snoopy*. The second day he complained because "everybody" had a Twinkie or a chocolate bar in his lunch, and all I had given Jack was a ginger cookie. The third day he said he was sick and tired of going to school in "matching" clothes, and he wanted to look "scroungy" like everybody else. The fourth day he complained about his nine-o'clock bedtime and said that nobody in the whole school had to go to bed before ten, except maybe those weirdos in kindergarten. And on Friday he said that the only way I could get him to wear his new white sneakers was if I let him drag his feet sideways all the way to school so they'd be good and dirty when he got there.

One thing about mutiny is that you usually get warnings. The gale signs had been posted since Monday, and by Friday we knew we'd have to do something.

In my own defense, I must add that I've always

let the kids choose their own lunch boxes as long as they eat what's in them. True, Twinkies and chocolate bars are a rare treat, not an everyday occurrence, but our kids don't have to subsist wholly on prune yogurt and granola, either. The "matching" clothes Jack was talking about were nothing more than plaid jeans and solid-colored shirts or vice versa, not co-ordinated cashmeres from Lord and Taylor's. Nine-o'clock bedtimes on school nights will be the rule until he is one year older, though I frequently make allowances for *National Geographic* specials. And finally, he has every right to scrape his feet sideways all the way to school as long as he buys the next pair of sneakers.

I sat down with Jack over the weekend. "You know perfectly well," I said, "that we won't let you do or have *anything* you want, but we do try to be reasonable. Tell me what would please you."

Jack thought it over, chin in hands, like a corporate executive contemplating a merger.

"One day a week," he decided, "ought to be 'Spoil-your-kid' day, and I should be able to wear what I want and eat what I want and go to bed whenever I please."

"You're on," I agreed. "Next Monday it is."

He took a long time preparing his lunch that morning. After thinking it over, he decided that maybe three Twinkies and a jelly sandwich were a bit much, so he took only two Twinkies and made the sandwich salami. He put on his oldest jeans and a dirty soccer shirt, but when he got a glimpse of himself in the mirror, he changed to a somewhat cleaner football jersey. And that night around 9:30, he remembered he had a math test the next day, so he lived it up for another fifteen minutes and then turned out the lights. S.Y.K. Day was, for all concerned, a huge success. It just goes to prove what Ralph and I have always believed: kids want to know you care about them. Give them a mile, sometimes, and they'll settle for an inch.

A CHANGE OF FEELINGS

When my children were mere infants, I used to look at their wee arms and legs, so helpless and vulnerable in their cribs, and vow that I would never let such small defenseless creatures outside alone on the sidewalk. Other parents might allow their toddlers to play within feet of a busy street, but never, ever, would I take that chance with my darlings.

Two years later we were strolling together out there on the sidewalk, my brood and I. Three years later I was merely watching from the porch. And when they had reached the grand old age of four, my wee helpless kids were on their own, within a few feet of a busy street.

Never, I told myself in one of my more fearful moments, would I allow my offspring to go out alone on Halloween. All sorts of things happened to children out there in the night—kidnappings, poisoned candy, razor blades in apples . . . Always I would be along to protect them, to snatch them away from the stranger's grasp, and hug them once more to my bosom.

"Aw, Mom, you're not coming along again this year, are you?" Jack grumbled at the advanced age of seven, and the mother who had promised to follow them about forever sat answering the doorbell instead.

I read about another car accident yesterday and found myself saying I would never allow my children to drive. If a squirrel ever ran in front of Susan at the wheel, she would go off the edge of a cliff before she would hit it. If Jack saw his best friend a block away, he would cut right across a corner lot to reach him. If Peter was driving on the freeway and got tired, I could envision his downy little head dropping lower and lower onto the steering wheel, and I broke out in perspiration just thinking about it.

But parenthood does have a bonus: perspective. I knew as soon as I'd thought it that four years from now Susan will be backing out our driveway. I knew that by the time Jack has a license, he will have completed a driver's education course that will make him more knowledgeable than I am. And finally, I knew that when Peter is finally behind the wheel, his head will no longer be downy. I will love him every bit as much as I do now, but I will love him in a different way.

Some parents wish their children would stay babies all their lives. As much as I love an infant, however, I am rather looking forward to wearing Susan's clothes, taking Jack's advice, and asking Peter to walk me home after dark.

OF TIME AND CHRISTMAS PAST

When I was small, a day was an interminable length of time stretching between breakfast and lunch and lunch and dinner. A year was a long succession of these days that seemed to last forever.

Strange what a few decades of birthdays will do to you. Now summer vacations are scarcely over before Thanksgiving is here, and twenty-four hours later it's Christmas. There are not enough minutes in the day to accomplish all I would love to do.

It seemed appalling to me, therefore, with work

always waiting at my fingertips, that a child with no obvious mental or physical defects should be whining that he was bored. That he should have repeated this five or six times during the course of one morning less than a week after Christmas—having opened nine different toys from assorted relatives—was beyond reason and sanity.

"You have nine wonderful presents . . ." I began, as Peter braced his back against the doorframe and started a slow descent to the floor, legs sliding out from under him.

"I've played with them all!" Peter protested. "There's a piece missing from the puzzle, the batteries in the truck are dead, and I'm tired of the rest. I want something different!"

It was also beyond reason and sanity and certainly the spirit of Christmas to feel such violence toward a child of mine.

"What about going over to Bobby's?" I asked, fighting for control.

"Bobby's on a trip with his uncle."

"Chris?"

"He doesn't like me any more."

Little wonder. There are times, however, when the still, small voice rescues our children from us and our tempers. Something told me to back off, to listen.

"What kind of thing do you think you might like?" I asked.

"Something with you—something we could do together," Peter said at once.

And there it was—so plain I wondered why I had missed it. It wasn't the tinsel and presents and glitter of Christmas that Peter wanted especially, but the feeling of closeness and sharing, and he obviously hadn't had enough.

I put down my manuscript and looked him in the eye.

"Peter," I said, "it's time we learned to make cinnamon buns." And two hours later we were still at it, flour up to the elbows, sharing something we hadn't had time to do in the rush of Christmas past.

PRESERVING THE SQUEAL

I was thinking about it yesterday when I looked out and saw the snow. A few years back, Peter would have stood at the top of the stairs, blinking out at the thick, white blanket, and bellowed, "Snow!" at the top of his lungs. And whoever was eating Wheat Chex at the breakfast table would have whispered, "Shhhh. The others are sleeping."

Peter does not bellow so loudly any more. He does not burst into our bedroom at six in the morning to announce his plans for the day or squeal that there's a squirrel on the bird feeder. He's learning.

Jack, too. It was six months ago when we finally cured him of leaping down a half flight of stairs when he was happy and trying to touch the ceiling of the family room, leaving fingerprints in his wake.

Even Susan had to have the savage weaned out of her. Bit by bit she learned to lower her voice, to subdue her exultations. She had to be taught that not everything that happened to her was world-shaking, and that a daisy growing up through a hole in the patio did not require an earsplitting squeal of delight.

Slowly we are teaching these children manners. Like young colts reprimanded for their friskiness, they are beginning to trot more sedately now, to whine rather than whinny. Day by day, week by week, a little of the spontaneity is replaced by order and duty and responsibility.

It's necessary, I suppose, but a little sad, too. Ralph once said that he hoped none of the children, no matter how cultivated, would ever "lose his squeal." That says it for both of us.

Voices must be lowered, I know, furniture cannot be jumped on, and screams must be reserved for the things in life that are really dramatic. But I hope that Peter never stands at the top of the stairs and says dully, "Snow." I hope Jack never loses his impulse to leap into the air and click his heels. I hope that a daisy pushing up miraculously through the concrete of the patio will always bring forth wonder, and that our children don't become so weighted down by worldly concerns that they cannot enjoy the quiet surprises of life.

That's why we occasionally look the other way when Jack descends the stairs six at a time. That's why we do not have a rule that voices must always, at all times, be restrained. We know the children will be trampled on at school by teachers, of necessity, and friends will tease them for their exuberance. But every so often, around our house, there's a long, loud bellow of delight, and it does our souls good to hear it.

THREE

The Private I

THE VENERATED AND THE VULNERABLE

I celebrate, if that's the word, my birthday this month. Everybody told me that thirty was absolutely the worst, and that once I had passed that year, the rest were a breeze.

Don't you believe it. Thirty didn't bother me at all. I looked in the mirror and couldn't see a bit of difference from when I was twenty. I felt more mature, I was more compassionate toward my fellowmen, and I knew I would live forever.

It's the succeeding birthdays that have bothered me. More and more I have begun to realize I do *not* perfectly resemble that young slip of a thing I was at twenty. I have gradually given up the idea of living forever, and my knees, which have "popped" since the age of nine, now seem to have a creak about them, too.

The children are well aware that I'm not wild about birthdays, at least not my own. And the more they try to be considerate and kind and understanding, the worse they make it.

Susan tried to keep the dinner conversation gracious. She launched into a tribute to my ability to make our house a real home, said how it was her most favorite place, and somehow wound up asking if we would be leaving the house to her when we . . . uh . . . passed on.

Jack instantly took over. He said it was marvelous the way I'd kept up my health for a woman of my age, and it was a good thing I didn't drink much, because alcohol kills brain cells, and he bet if I were a lush, I'd hardly have any cells left at all.

I could almost feel my degenerative processes taking over. There are times I wish I were an old Chinese grandmother—venerated, adored—sitting cross-legged before my rice bowl, dispensing advice to appreciative relatives.

"It's okay, Mom," Peter said, squeezing onto my chair beside me as I prepared to blow out my thousands of candles. "When you're *really* old, you can be a grandmother and have fun all over again!"

Now that's positive thinking for you. That's approaching middle age with joy—glee, even. Susan, Jack, and Peter, reproduce yourselves as soon as possible, please. With kids like these around, how could old age ever catch up with me? I'll be so busy staying one step ahead of them that I won't even have time to think about it.

KEEPING MUM

The most difficult prohibitions in the Bible are not the Ten Commandments, but that bit about not letting the right hand know what the left hand is up to. The hardest thing in the world is to do something good and noble, and then shut up about it.

This year I made a secret resolution that every day I would do something a little extra for somebody without telling them. Every day I would go out of my way to do a small kindness which I would keep to myself.

The first day I pressed all the trousers in Ralph's closet. The second day I took all those little stubs of pencils that Peter carries back and forth to school and sharpened them for him. The third day I fixed the loose fender on Jack's bicycle, and the fourth day I transplanted Susan's geranium into a larger pot.

Four days. That's all it lasted. The morning after I'd pressed Ralph's pants, I sat on the edge of the bed while he dressed and waited for the adulation and gratitude that were my due. At seven in the morning, however, it's all Ralph can do to see through the creases of his eyes, much less notice the crease of his pants, and, of course, he said nothing.

Peter went blithely off to school with a fistful of newly sharpened pencils without even a glimmer of surprise. Jack went whizzing off to the library on a bike that no longer rattled without so much as a glance at his back fender. And on the fourth day, when I found Susan watering her geranium without even a word of acknowledgment about the new pot, my maturity crumbled like a raisin cookie.

Not only did I tell the family all I had done for them, but I told them about the resolution, too. They were sorry all right—for me.

"Boy, you really blew it, Mom!" said Susan.

"Better luck next time," said Jack.

"Try it again when you're a little older," Peter suggested.

If I wait until I'm fifty and try again, do you think I'll be able to swing it?

OF TIME AND GEORGE WASHINGTON'S BIRTHDAY

I don't know how it is in your part of the country, but here next to the nation's capital, George Washington's birthday is almost as revered as Christmas.

Coming as I did from the Midwest, where the only thing we did on GWB was cut out red paper hatchets in first grade, I experienced cultural shock when I got to Maryland. George Washington's birthday is the occasion for the greatest sale of the year everywhere from department stores to hamburger stands. Shopping centers offer free cherry pies to the first one-hundred people; business-machine stores offer typewriters for ten dollars to the first five customers who enter the door. Every commercial establishment has a gimmick, and if George Washington himself had known what would go on, he probably would have thrown that silver dollar into the Potomac and then himself.

As it is, people with sleeping bags begin camping outside the doors so they can be the first to get a typewriter. Parking spaces are nonexistent, traffic is tied up for miles, and if someone yelled "fire" in a bargain basement, he'd be arrested.

Consequently, George Washington's birthday is the one day of the year I don't venture outside my door. A minute saved is one-sixtieth of an hour, and I can think of a thousand things I'd rather do with my hour than camp outside Kresge's waiting for a cherry pie.

I'm one of those hopeless time-savers who can't go upstairs without taking something with me or bringing something down, who never goes to the store without making a list of all the chores I could do on the way back. Shopping is limited to once a week, ironing to every other week, and we all have enough underwear to survive three weeks on a desert island without my doing laundry.

And yet, admirable as I may seem to my hardy ancestors who used to get up at 4 A.M. and do half a day's work before breakfast, I wonder sometimes if the saving of minutes, like the saving of pennies, doesn't become an end in itself—the frantic race to do tomorrow's work today, to beat the deadline, to get a jump on next week, and fling oneself madly into the month ahead.

Every so often, something tells me to stop. It tells me to put my work aside, lean back, and take a child on my lap. And because I don't want to wake up some day and discover that the children are gone and life has passed me by, the kids and I kick off our shoes, settle down, and talk about cabbages and kings.

WHO'S ON FIRST?

Last night I put a new dish on the table. It consisted of pork chops, turnips, and applesauce and was, I thought, rather good.

Now, I learned long ago that a recipe called "Turnip Surprise" will only terrify my brood. So I renamed it "Three-Ring Circus" or something and thought I was home free. Just as Susan picked up her fork, however, she asked, "Have you ever made this dish before?" and I said I had not. That set off the alarm button. For the rest of the meal three forks were busily picking and dissecting and examining every piece as though they might find fried beetles beneath the sauce.

What is it, do you suppose, that frightens people about "first times"? If I tell Ralph I have an appointment in an unfamiliar part of town he will say, "But you've never driven there before." When Peter had his eyes tested and Jack's teacher assigned a theme, the boys bleated, "But they never asked for that before." And when Susan saw me wearing a pair of red tights beneath my plaid skirt one winter morning she gasped, "Mo—other! I never saw you in red tights before!"

What's happened to the spirit of adventure? I would like to know. There's got to be a first time for everything. Every idea, every voyage, every invention, every symphony or painting or story didn't just ooze into place by osmosis. *Someone* had to start the ball rolling. *Somebody* took that first step.

It's possible, of course, that a dish called "Turnip Surprise" could taste like trash. It's possible that I might drive across town and become hopelessly lost. It's even possible that if I go to the supermarket in

73]

red tights the manager will ask why I'm not in school, though I rather doubt it.

But I think my family needs a little shaking. I think that once a week each of us should try out a new idea or project that he has never tried before, just to get in the habit because, when the right moment comes along, I don't want my kids to be afraid to reach for something big, something far beyond red tights and a Turnip Surprise.

NEW TRICKS, OLD DOGS

Anybody who managed to get through the swinging sixties and the selfish seventies with herself, her psyche, and her marriage intact deserves a bonus. It's enough that she has to keep her kids off drugs and do her share of the income tax and try to memorize the new lists of carcinogenic foods that appear weekly in the paper. She should not have to take on any additional burdens. She should not, in short, at this stage of life, have to learn the metric system as well.

When I told Ralph I simply could not learn it, that I wouldn't know a "kill-oh-meter" if it fell on me, he said, "What do you mean, 'learn it'? You can't even pronounce it."

What are they trying to do to us, anyway? We are the parents who struggled through the new math only to discover that all the new terms we'd so diligently learned to help Susan are now being slowly eased out as Jack and Peter make the scene. We know the elephant jokes by heart, the knock-knock jokes, the names of the rock groups, the names of the teachers—even the lists of enemies and friends, which are subject to change daily. How am I supposed to learn the metric system as well?

What about us slow learners? I was twenty before I was positively sure how many feet there were in a mile—thirty before I knew all about tablespoons, teaspoons, thirds, halves, and pints. If somebody takes away my inches and feet, my first major gaffe will be to walk in the store and order a kilometer of coffee, or tell someone that our house is three liters away from the library.

Ralph says they'll let old dogs like us take it slowly, but I can already see those centimeters crawling into my house. Already Peter's got a metric ruler. Jack bought a new speedometer with nary a mile on it, and Susan reports that everything in her home-economics class is measured in liters and such.

We, in our middle years, need something to call our own. Take away the Big Band sounds and "Star Dust," if you must. Take away Greer Garson and Walter Pidgeon. Take, if you must, those large shady porches where we used to spend so many summer evenings. And when I die, dig my grave in kilometers, if you must, but let me at least go under with a one-foot ruler in my hand as a final measure of defiance.

A GRACEFUL GROWING

A terrible thing happened last week. Ralph and I went to a dinner party, and I didn't realize until I got home that the sole topic of conversation had been health. We started out with somebody's horror story of a wonder drug that caused deafness, moved on to a discussion of hospitals, graduated to diets and the power of positive thinking, and ended up diagnosing each other's joint pains. The awful thing was that I wasn't bored.

I'm getting old, I told myself, staring at my face in the mirror. Ten years ago I would have refused to go to a party where guests were no more interesting than that. Five years ago, even, I would have found an excuse to leave early. But there I was discussing ligaments with the best of them.

Since when had I developed lines on either side of my mouth? Was my chin beginning to sag, or was it just my imagination? Had that little mole always been on my right cheek, and . . . merciful heavens . . . there were five distinct silver hairs on the top of my head, not two. Was it all right to pull them out, or was that a prelude to going bald? Was I getting larger about the hips? When had I measured last? And my hands . . . good grief, my hands . . . !

"What's the matter, Mother?" Susan asked, stopping by my room.

"I'm growing old, Susan," I mumbled.

"Everybody's growing older all the time, Mom," she said, plunking herself down on the bed. "Daddy, Peter, Jack, me, the Queen of England. So what else is new?"

"But I hate it, Susan!" I protested, as though she could stop the aging process if I begged hard enough.

Susan lay back and studied me as only a twelve-going-on-thirteen-year-old daughter can.

"Well, Mother," she said finally, "you've got two choices: you can either go kicking and screaming into middle age and become an old shrew that everybody hates, or you can grow old gracefully so that men will still go mad over you when you're ninety-nine."

Why is it that a child who chews bubble gum and giggles and says nutty things to boys can also be a well of profundity upon occasion? Instantly my mind was filled with women I had known who fit both descriptions perfectly, and I knew which choice I wanted to make. The only thing that would keep me attractive and lovable, yea, even on into my nineties, was to stay loving myself. I was here for a better purpose than sitting in front of the mirror searching for wrinkles. And so, bolstered by the philosophical musings of my young daughter, I put on my coat and went outside to see if the daffodils were poking up yet.

A SECRET LUST

Everybody, they say, has at least one secret peculiarity, some closet quirk that stays hidden even from loved ones.

Well, mine isn't very secret. The entire family knows I am addicted to chocolate, and that the presence of a mere Milky Way in the house can set me off. They know that once this ordinarily sane and sensible woman gets a taste of that silky stuff on her tongue, it takes the Foreign Legion to make her stop.

I know how I got this way, but it doesn't help. When I was five, a relative gave my eight-year-old sister a large chocolate Easter rabbit. He gave me nothing. Because the creature was all decorated in pink and yellow tin foil, and we were unused to such things during the Depression, my sister decided not to eat it right away, but keep it on her dresser to savor and admire.

Week after week I passed that rabbit with feelings of jealousy and desire. There he sat, his chocolate decomposing, slowly going stale. It was just too much to take.

And so one day, in a fit of insanity, I grabbed that chocolate animal, sat at the top of the stairs, and began to eat—the ears first.

When my sister came home from school fifteen minutes later, I was down to the pink and yellow tin foil around the feet. She stared at me incredulously and then, screaming with rage, grabbed a pair of scissors off the dresser and cut off a huge hunk of my hair.

I knew I had it coming, though the punishment didn't quite seem to fit the crime. My stomach was full, my face was smeared, and a five-year-old girl couldn't care less that she was bald on the back of her head.

To this day, though, when I see chocolate—especially pure, thick milk chocolate—I get an uncontrollable lust for it. Place chocolate candy anywhere in my house and I hear it calling me. Hide it, and I still spend an entire day searching for it. I am beyond rehabilitation.

It is something to remember when I expect Susan, Jack, and Peter to show more self-control. No mother can really scold a son for making a flying tackle at his brother when she herself, just that morning, did the same thing over a ten-cent bar of chocolate.

FOR ME, WITH LOVE

It is, I'd always thought, bad manners to refuse a gift
—a gift given out of love with no strings attached.
That's why, when my family announced on Mother's
Day Eve that I could expect breakfast in bed the
following morning, I did not object.

I'll admit, the very thought was profoundly dis-
concerting. I had never had breakfast in bed in my
life, unless you counted my stays in the hospital for
childbirth. So I got out my twelve-year-old bed jacket,
laid it beside my pillow in anticipation, and went to
sleep dreaming of a bamboo tray with the morning
paper folded neatly on one side and a rose on the
other, and in between, on a porcelain plate, eggs
benedict and some hot blueberry muffins slathered
with butter.

I overslept the next morning, dimly aware that
the rest of the family was up and doing something
down in the kitchen. Fifteen minutes later I bolted
upright as the smell of burned eggs filled the house,
and I could hear Peter exclaiming disgustedly, "Open
the windows! Open the windows!" I did not go back
to sleep.

There seemed to be an unusual amount of clattering and clanking of pans which I could not understand. They were not, after all, making Thanksgiving dinner, only eggs benedict or . . . uh . . . perhaps a mere omelet. Something crashed to the floor, and I heard Ralph say in exasperation, "Not the orange juice!"

I sat up, put on my bed jacket, and ran a comb through my hair. At last footsteps sounded in the hall and Peter appeared bearing a saucer with one dry, cold piece of toast.

"Happy Mother's Day," he chirped. "The rest will be up in a minute. This is the part I made."

"Thank you, Peter," I said.

He waited. "Did you want anything on it?" he asked finally.

"Well, why don't you surprise me?"

He took the toast downstairs again and returned it smeared with peanut butter.

Ten minutes later, five minutes after the toast was gone, Susan came in with a metal tray bearing a fried egg and a cup of coffee. She had forgotten the fork and napkin and had to go back down. "Happy Mother's Day," she said. "Dad's still squeezing the oranges."

Fifteen minutes later a glass of juice was delivered by a husband whose smile seemed a bit artificial. And when the last of the coffee was gone, Jack remembered the morning paper.

"Did you enjoy your breakfast, Mom?" Peter

asked later, when I finally contemplated getting up.

Is there a synonym for enjoy that conveys appreciation but not pleasure?

"We cleaned up the whole kitchen afterwards," Jack added. "Everything's back where it was . . . finally."

"I enjoyed it very much," I said, with complete honesty now. Half the fun of any meal is knowing that nothing awaits you in the sink.

OF FEET AND FOLLY

It is necessary, I know, to have rules. It is important for children to respect property. But I wonder about our sense of values.

When we bought our house, we inherited a light-gray rug which covers the living room, dining room, hall, and stairs. The previous owner must not have had children. In fact, he must not have had feet. One can hardly step outside to pick up the newspaper without depositing a big dusty footprint on the carpet when coming back in. The rug, consequently, was a study in gray and black within a month of our arrival.

Once it had been cleaned, the children were threatened with infanticide should they dirty it again.

"Take off your shoes!" I would bellow as soon as they opened the front door, and we rapidly reached the point where sneakers were kicked off the instant a child entered. So well was our brood conditioned that neighbors reported our children played in their homes shoeless.

Because two hassocks had been worn out by rolling and wrestling, we charged the children a dime each time we found them sitting/laying/rolling on the new one. Likewise rules and fines for eating on the carpet, feet on the sofa, and chewing gum left on the coffee table.

"Don't tip the chairs!" Ralph used to say sternly, after Peter's squirming, wriggling, and tipping at mealtimes had caused one of the chair legs to fall off. And then one evening I counted and discovered that the conversation had been interrupted eleven times to admonish Peter to sit still.

I don't know. I think I have been mistaking the rug for holy ground. I have made an altar of the furniture and sacrificed my children's spontaneity on it. I have greeted them each day after school with, "Take off your shoes!" instead of, "How did it go today?"

The great thing about life is that you can change, and I am now unlearning my behavior. The children are not cautioned about shoes except when the ground is muddy. Peter is not scolded *every* time he tips back in his chair, and I have decided to let the

83]

hassock go the way of all hassocks—for how many years do my boys have left to roll about the family room like bear cubs?

I have resolved in the days ahead to put faith, hope, and charity back where they belong, and to demote the furniture far down the list.

RETREAT

Jack has decided he needs privacy—a place to call his own. The top half of a set of bunk beds, he tells me, is not enough. He wants a hideout, a nook, a cranny where, when the door is shut or the curtain drawn, he will be assured of peace and quiet, a place where he can hibernate at will in the embryonic state.

Not having an attic room or a nook or even a cranny that would hold a ten-year-old boy, we suggested a large box from a warehouse, but Jack devised his own solution. The space beneath the Ping-Pong table in the basement, he declared, was now officially his. He taped old sheets around the edges of the table, giving it the appearance of a makeshift stage for a down-at-the-heels politician. Inside these sheeted walls he dragged his sleeping bag, a box of cookies, a flashlight, a jar of water, a study lamp and a stack of comic books—and called it home.

It hasn't done much for the basement, but it's done wonders for Jack, who races to his hideaway the minute he gets home from school and retreats there once more after dinner. I managed to smuggle a few *National Geographics* in among his comic books and contributed a wildlife poster to hang at one end, but other than that, we let him be. Whatever Jack is working out, he's doing it in his own way, and I can think of a lot worse.

In fact, I've been looking around a little myself. We could all use a little lean-to now and then—a cave, a cocoon, a womb to engulf us and hold us fast. We all need a place where, when the curtains are shut, no one dares disturb us.

I could drape a bedspread over the ironing board, I suppose, and sit under there when the going gets tough. I could hang a beach towel from the middle drawer of my desk and crawl in the space behind. I could, if I tried hard enough, climb up on my closet shelf and curl up in the fetal position: let the telephone ring, the doorbell chime, the kids go from room to room calling my name, nobody would ever think of looking for me on my closet shelf, and through a crack in the door, I could survey my family doing without me and wish them well.

I'm not sure whether, in the stillness of my closet, I'd have any profound revelations, but if I ever manage to get up on that shelf and give it a try, I'll let you know.

FOR THE LOVE OF
SEPTEMBER

Do they sense it, do you suppose? As August draws to a close, do my children know that I await September breathlessly, that I welcome it, and the start of school, with open arms? Do they know that I long for a quiet house, an orderly schedule, and the time to take up the many projects I left unfinished in June?

They sense it.

"You act like you're *happy* about it," Peter grouses over his toast as he contemplates his final week of freedom.

"I look forward to *every* month," I say, skirting the issue. "Each one has its own special flavor."

"The flavor of September is *ugh*," says Jack.

"The leaves start to turn," I remind him.

"So does my stomach," puts in Susan dryly.

They aren't being entirely honest either, I realize. By August, summer has become a bit of a bore, but they would die rather than admit it. Every so often a wistful comment slips out like "I wonder if Ted Parker will be in my room again this year," or "Sam and I are going to walk together on the first day."

I try to restrain my enthusiasm. I try not to lay out their school clothes more than a day in advance, and I never go shopping for notebooks and paste and rulers until they have brought home a list of essentials. Still, under my breath, I am urging August on and mentally marking off the days on the calendar.

It's not that I don't love them, these kids. I have heard of mothers who say they cry when the children leave for school and sit around waiting for three o'clock. That's not me. I love them more, I've discovered, when they're not around all the time—when there are plenty of spaces in our togetherness.

The moment the last child is out the door, I go into a sort of frenzied round dance. Clothes are picked up, beds made, dishes stacked, and by the time Peter has reached the playground, I have tended to the house and am ready to tackle whatever is waiting on my desk.

Maybe it works because they know I'm glad to see them again. Maybe they tolerate my September enthusiasm because they know they are welcome at home once more—once I've had my breathing time. Maybe they sense that once I have tucked my muse away for the day, I am ready for children and chatter and an evening of fun. And maybe they'll even forgive me if I slip up some time and say, "Only three more days till school!"

A MOMENTARY REGRESSION

Susan caught me weeping the other day in a rare moment of loneliness.

"Mo—ther!" she gasped. "You're crying!"

"Of course," I told her. "I'm homesick. But I'll be over it in a few minutes."

She stood there gaping at me. "How can you be homesick when you're *home?*" she insisted. And when I explained that I missed her aunts and uncles and sole surviving grandparent, she looked genuinely alarmed and said, "I didn't know mothers ever cried."

What did she think I was, that girl of mine? Did she suppose that tear ducts, like arteries, become clogged over the years?

Just because a woman has children doesn't mean she never feels pain at the dentist's or misses her father or feels inadequate and insecure, I told Susan. Just because a man is on the advisory board of the local library and weighs one-hundred-eighty pounds does not mean he is never childish or frightened or unreasonable.

It's strange, though, how we try to disguise feelings, even in things we write. Somehow in the cold factual light of reports and summaries, words seem to take the emotion out of situations. Infidelities, jealousies, and resentments between husband and wife are simply referred to as "marital problems." Vicious street fighting with knives and chains is referred to as a "disturbance." Children seething with hostility are said to have "adjustment difficulties," and families that have to resort to dog food to stay alive are said to be in "economic straits."

I was thinking about hidden emotions the other day as I lay stretched out on the doctor's examining table waiting for my yearly checkup. A Gauguin print looked gently down on me from the wall on the left. Pictures, drawn by the doctor's children, smiled happily from the wall on the right. Muzak floated out from a speaker in the corner, and a vase of artificial roses decorated the desk.

Did the doctor really think, I wondered, that the pink plastic flowers would make me forget the discomfort of the instruments? Did he imagine that the children's happy pictures would make me oblivious to the hardness of the table, or that the Muzak would put me in a state of bliss until the examination was over? How many other women had lain beneath the soundproof ceiling, repressing the urge to scream at the Gauguin print? How many other women had desperately wanted to kick over the vase of roses or attack the speaker in the corner? Had anybody ever done a study?

Just when unspeakable feelings inside me began to take over, the doctor came in, washed his hands, remarked on the weather, and asked about my children. Suddenly I was my supposedly mature self once more, and Susan would be glad to know I had not thrown a fit and fallen off the table.

CHANGE

When I was very young, I used to worry about growing up. I thought of all the things I enjoyed that my parents didn't and wondered if age would have the same effect on me. I made a pact with myself that no matter what happened, I would never grow tired of reading the comics, or hanging from the trapeze by my knees. Life is fickle. I've already stopped hanging by my knees.

As another year approaches, I wonder about myself and my resistance to change. I'm not alone in this, of course. Ralph has resisted buying a new front door for so long that now we automatically give directions by saying, "The house with the warped blue door." Even worse, Ralph has become so attached to that malformation that he doesn't ever want to replace it. He says nobody will be able to find our house if he does.

It's remarkable, really, how we stick to our old ways and stand up for our own failings—how we go on justifying our unkindnesses rather than trying to change ourselves. How often, I wonder, have I yelled at Peter to stop his shouting? Or exploded at Jack because he lost his temper once too often? Or made a snide comment to Susan about her sarcasm? How often have I asked far more of Ralph than I, in turn, could give? It's all too easy to go on reacting in the same old way because, were we to admit we've been wrong or unwise or unkind, we'd have to face the damage we've done.

I sometimes wonder whether I would like myself if we met on the street. Would I think, "Now that's a woman I'd like to know," impressed by my vitality and cheerfulness?

I don't know. I stood in front of the mirror just now and didn't feel any great enthusiasm. "That's a woman," I thought, "who could stand to lose a good five pounds. Why on earth does she wear her hair that way, and how long has it been since she's laughed?"

Perhaps, when Ralph gets home from work, he will find a new me—or the start of a new me—or at least the motivation to be a new me. Inch by inch we become the person we would truly like to be—beginning now.

A LEARNING SITUATION

Yesterday I behaved abominably toward my children. Discovering that I had cut out a pattern on the wrong side of fabric costing $6.98 a yard, I raged at the slightest provocation and made life miserable for all concerned. In fact, I made life intolerable for the unconcerned as well, since my children had no more to do with my sewing disaster than the weather in Nebraska.

By evening, I knew that an apology was in order. Like the prodigal son returning home to say, "I have sinned against heaven and in thy sight," I went upstairs, where the boys were plotting against me.

Jack looked down warily from the top bunk as I opened my prodigal mouth.

"I just want to say that I've been in a terrible mood today because my sewing didn't go right. You boys had nothing to do with it, and I'm sorry I've been so cross and unreasonable."

The boys thought this over in silence. I should have known that there is no fatted calf for a repentant mother, however humble.

"Do we get any candy?" asked Peter.

"What do you mean?"

"Well, if you're sorry and everything, you ought to give us candy."

I replied that an apology should be sufficient, and that the truly charitable thing to do was forgive without asking for compensation.

"She's right," Jack agreed. "She ought to be punished, but she shouldn't have to give us anything."

I was clinging desperately to the last shreds of my humility. "A Christian doesn't ask for penalties, either," I insisted.

"Then how come I have to do something nice for Peter after I pound him?" Jack demanded.

"That's our way of teaching you to be considerate of others—it's a learning situation, not a punishment," I insisted; but even before I said it, I knew they had me.

According to Luke, the prodigal son got the best robes and shoes on his feet and a ring on his hand, all because he said he was sorry. I got two hours in the kitchen making a chocolate pie, which the boys decided would teach me to be more considerate.

FOUR

The Nesting Process

MISTAKEN IDENTITY

It seems very strange, but the way to live an anonymous life is to spend it in an apartment. Until we bought a house ten years ago, no one but relatives and editors knew where we lived. Suddenly, when we were installed in our own little one-fourth of an acre, we became known to hundreds of people who had us pegged as millionaires.

During the first week at our new address, we got a call from a developer wanting us to buy a beach house at the ocean. With 288 mortgage payments to look forward to, see, he wants us to buy another house as well. The reasoning must be that people who buy one plot of land are starting a collection, because as soon as the beach developer hung up, the cemetery called and asked if we were interested in a family plot.

In less than two weeks, we'd had four salesmen wanting to put a new roof on our house and attach new aluminum siding and gutters. Others wanted to check our furnace, inspect us for termites, and waterproof the basement. Did they know something about our house that we didn't?

But that wasn't the worst. Up until then our mail had consisted mostly of bills, correspondence from editors, and rejected manuscripts. Suddenly we were receiving those little catalogs that advertise back scratchers, mixing bowls, and beach towels, and the number of mailings doubled every Tuesday.

Now I realize that charitable organizations sell their list of contributors to other organizations whose goals are similar. And if you buy handmade goods from a shop in North Carolina, you'll get a brochure from West Virginia as well.

But how did we get on a list for nautical supplies when we've never owned a rowboat? Why do we get catalogs advertising boots, saddles, and horse blankets, not to mention bar supplies and orthopedic equipment?

Jung believed in a collective unconscious, in which everything the human race had learned was filed away, available to sensitive individuals who could dip into it. I'm sure he was right. Only it's not unconscious knowledge at all that's in the public domain—it's addresses and phone numbers, and the only thing one needs to hook onto it is a license to sell real estate, funeral plots, or horse blankets.

FAMILY OF THE YEAR

At breakfast, Jack announced that he was the only boy in his church school class who would get a gold pin for perfect attendance throughout the year.

Peter figured out that he had missed only two Sundays, one for chicken pox and one for five stitches on the forehead when he fell up the church steps (don't ask me how a six-year-old can fall *up* the steps, but Peter did).

"If there was an award for 'Family of the Year' or something, I'd bet we'd get it," Jack boasted.

I stared at my offspring over the scrambled eggs. If they got along any worse than they did, we'd have to keep them in separate cages. How could they possibly be so puffed up?

Ralph shared my sentiments exactly because he said, "An award like that would have to be for more than warming a pew every Sunday, you know. What about cooperation and brotherhood and—" He got no further.

Jack glared across the table at Peter. "We could win it easy if it weren't for crybaby Peter."

99]

"If it wasn't for you pounding my head all the time, you mean," retorted a mouthful of toast and jelly.

"The only way this family could get an award would be for you two guys to drop dead," said Susan in a gross distortion of the Christian ethic. "But I bet I could get one for Bible reading."

"Yeah?" yelped Jack. "Then who's Nebuchadnezzar?"

"Easy!" said Susan. "Who's Hagar?"

"Easy!" said Jack. "Who's Mishma? Huh? Who's Mishma?"

"The Sunday School superintendent?" guessed Peter.

Ralph retreated to the editorial page, and I carted the dishes out to the kitchen. I tried to envision our family ever receiving a "Family of the Year" award. I doubted we'd even make it up on stage. Peter would fall up the steps, naturally, and Jack would pound him for doing it. Susan would burst into tears at the behavior of her brothers, and Ralph and I would try to look detached.

No, I decided, it would be like giving a cannibal the "Vegetarian of the Year" award. We had a long way to go before we reached the serenity of that little family in Nazareth.

But who on earth was Mishma?

WALDEN IN THE MAKING

Probably because I feel guilty that we have no dog or cat, I gave Peter a frog-hatching kit for his birthday. Don't ask me how I thought a frog would substitute for a cuddly warm pup, but I figured that anything that moved and breathed would at least convince Peter I didn't have a grudge against life.

For two months the tadpoles lived and moved and had their being in the large bowl of my Mixmaster. As they increased in wisdom and stature and favor with neighborhood kids, I aged their daily change of water in a bucket in the backyard so that it would develop just the right amount of algae.

I began to get concerned. Somehow I had the idea they should long since have become frogs. I examined them daily for signs of forelegs and finally called a scientist in desperation. We had the kind of tadpoles, he told me, that take a year to develop. I realized that my Mixmaster was off limits indefinitely.

It was then I decided on a simple little pond under the lilac bush, a place where the tadpoles could take care of themselves and feed off the hapless bugs that fell in their water. Why hadn't I thought of this before? Ralph said it was okay with him as long as the pond didn't become a cesspool, so I got a book at the library and read up. Lesson #1: There is no such thing as a simple pond.

On Monday I drove out in the country to buy a galvanized washtub, the kind our grandmothers used. On Tuesday I gave it a special scrubbing with vinegar to neutralize the zinc. On Wednesday I bought a can of white epoxy paint to coat the inside, but the man at the aquarium said I'd be better off with the color of algae, so I exchanged it on Thursday. On Friday I painted the tub and let it set over the weekend.

The following Monday I went to a hardware store and bought a bag of special sand. On Tuesday I purchased plants and snails from the aquarium. On Wednesday I added the dechlorinated water, which had been aging in buckets all over the backyard. On Thursday we put in the biggest tadpole, Mo, and when he proved to be alive on Friday, we added Eenie, Meenie, and Minie. And because I'd gone to so much trouble, I decided to splurge and toss in a couple of goldfish as well.

Every day we go out and aerate the water by displacing scoopfuls. Every day we feed the fish and skim leaves off the top.

I mean, how much is a tadpole's life worth? At what point do you decide that your budget is more important than a croak in the night? To Peter, who sits by the pond every day, dangling one hand in the water, it is worth an entire summer of dreams.

GOD'S LITTLE 1/32 OF AN ACRE

There is something satisfying about a garden, and anyone who has ever eaten so much as a bean that he planted himself knows that it tastes infinitely better than any bean anywhere else in the world. Every year, therefore, I have planted a little garden outside our study window, and I enjoy looking up from my desk to peer through two rows of corn to see what the children are doing in the yard.

Yes, corn. The neighbors said it couldn't be done. Our instincts told us we shouldn't even attempt it. My father, who was raised in the Midwest, mused that farmers in Iowa would throw corn like ours to the pigs. But we have savored each crooked kernel and congratulated ourselves on our finesse.

This year, however, the garden was a disaster. The four tomato plants grew so rapidly and so thick that they virtually attacked us when we walked out the back door, and then they produced a total of only six tomatoes. The beets looked like radishes, the lima beans wilted and died, and the asparagus peeped up

103]

from the ground and promptly disappeared.

After all my work, I thought bitterly. After spending $2.30 for seeds, an hour or so spading, a few minutes a day watering and weeding, how dare the vegetables mutiny in August! How dare they make us start September with only one bacon-and-tomato sandwich under our belts! What's the matter, God? Here we are, trying to be fruitful and multiply, and we can't even get a decent helping of lima beans!

Then I remembered my grandfather and the agonies he suffered. If my corn fails, I simply go to the produce stand and pick up a few ears for supper. If my grandfather's crop failed, it spelled economic catastrophe. There would be no money to repair the roof that winter, no money to buy another cow, no money for shoes for the seven children who would need them for school in the autumn. Each day the weather forecast was practically a matter of life or death, and I can still remember his drawn face as he looked out over his parched fields, watching for a cloud that might signal the end of a two-week drought.

May I never forget how easy my life is in comparison. When I pack my children's lunches this year, may I remember that the wheat for the flour did not come easily, that the cow which produced the butter was fussed over by somebody, and that if I have any sense at all, I will get the advice of a seasoned gardener before I play farmer again next year.

GOING HOME

A few weeks ago, we drove out to Illinois for a family reunion, the first in fifteen years. One contingent arrived from Florida, another from Oregon, and we represented the East Coast.

As the corn fields rolled by, I was overwhelmed with nostalgia and coaxed Ralph into making a detour through southern Indiana to look up the old homesteads (there were six of them).

Thomas Wolfe, you were right when you said, "You can't go home again." You were talking about the changes in oneself, I know, but I was appalled by the changes in those places I once loved. The first one we found was an empty lot, with only the steps and walk remaining of what used to be a large Victorian house with a mulberry tree in the backyard. The others had deteriorated to an alarming degree, and one (which had been part grocery store when my father owned it during the Depression) was now a shop for women's clothes.

How dare they tinker with my past? How dare they turn a grocery store, with all its fragrant memories, into a garment shop! How dare they tear down a home I loved or change the color of another or build a garage where our garden used to be!

What will my children find, I wonder, when they try to come back to our own house thirty years hence? Will their favorite climbing tree be gone? Will someone have cut down the swing? Will future occupants have taken out the little pond we so lovingly created, or subdivided the rooms, or put a door where no door should be?

The only sure thing about life is that there will be change, and it's hard, sometimes, for me to accept that. There will not only be changes in my house, but in my children and husband as well.

May I grow along with them. May I always be open to their becoming what is best for them. And may my azalea bushes always remain by the back fence, no matter what else new owners may do to my house.

THE NIGHT THE LIGHTS WENT OUT

Last Thursday I had a million things to do. I had an assignment to finish, a proof to read, a letter to type, a pie to bake, a shirt to iron, and one last load of clothes for the dryer. There was also a program on public television I had circled on the calendar.

I was flying around the house, giving orders and slinging papers and making everybody anxious, when there was a roll of thunder and a rush of hail and rain. It was as though I had made not only my children tense but the Almighty as well. All around us limbs were cracking off trees and shingles were blowing off houses. When the storm was over, we counted thirteen huge trees down in one block alone, and the electricity was off over the whole area.

Any minute now, we told ourselves, the lights will come back on. An hour, maybe. Two at the most. But when we finally got through to the power company, they said it would be morning at the earliest, possibly a day or two. Three hundred lines were down and they were working as fast as they could.

We went for a walk and talked to the neighbors. We got in the car and took a drive. We sent out for Chinese food and ate it by candlelight. I sat down at the piano not for ten minutes but for almost an hour. We played about a dozen hands of Hearts, told stories, bathed by candlelight, and went to bed.

I did not bake a pie, read a proof, watch TV, type a letter, or iron. And the world did not end. There *was* time for the family after all. There was time for laughter and fun and stories and music, and since the power did not come on until late the following night, we did it all over again.

A FAMILY AFFAIR

I know that when a child needs psychotherapy, it's advisable to treat the whole family. I know that when the boss bawls out the husband, the husband takes it out on his wife who takes it out on the kids who take it out on the dog who bites the mailman who goes home and takes it out on his wife, ad infinitum. I know there are neuroses that run through every family, and that they hang around for years.

One of the ways a counselor works through marital problems is to force his client to look at himself. A man who complains that his wife is a shrew will be asked what kind of a man would marry an ill-tempered nag. A woman who objects because her husband is aloof and unresponsive will be asked what kind of woman would marry a cold, unaffectionate man. When the client delves into questions like these, he realizes that marriage is a two-way street, that neurosis is a family affair, and that we often subconsciously choose what we really want, like it or not.

Can one apply the same test, I wonder, to children? Can one ask oneself what kind of mother would have a daughter who never picks up her clothes? Or what kind of father would have sons who argue endlessly over who gets the blue cup for breakfast?

Whether Susan, Jack, and Peter have more than their share of childhood anxieties, I'm not sure, but the ones they picked are real winners. What do you say, for example, when a six-year-old complains that bubbles of spit in his mouth keep him awake at night? Where do you start—with a tongue depressor and a flashlight, or with a talk on physiology? What do you do when a ten-year-old son constantly pulls at the collar of his shirt because he can't stand it touching his neck, no matter what shirt he puts on? What do you say to a pre-teenage daughter who always walks with her arms bent so that no one can see her elbows?

What did we do, Ralph wondered aloud the other night, to produce such hang-ups? Is there a streak of pathology running through the family? Will the children get more nervous and nutty as time goes on? And suddenly, as we talked, I remembered a time in third grade when I always touched everything twice. My touch, I fantasized, was actually a person whom I left standing on the table or the dresser or whatever, and since it would be a shame to leave him there alone, I always added another.

Did it lead to claustrophobia or schizophrenia? No. Did I get over it? Yes.

"This too shall pass," I said to Ralph; for the

problems of childhood have a way of working themselves out and being replaced by others far worse.

SHERLOCK'S HOME

With all this knowledge of body language and games
people play, it should come as a surprise to no one
that we communicate with each other without even
opening our mouths.

I submit that any family who's made it through
fifteen years together learns things about each other
through a kind of osmosis. Susan calls it prying, Jack
calls it snooping, Peter calls it sticking your nose in
somebody's business; but I say it's just plain detective
work that comes easily if you're a fair observer of
human behavior—especially if the humans are your
own family.

I know when the children have been snacking by
the amount they eat for dinner. I know when Jack
has had a bad day at school by the way he goes im-
mediately to his room. I know when Susan is talking
to a boy on the telephone by the way she giggles, and
it is obvious when Peter has tracked mud on the rug
because he instantly begins wailing, "I'm sorry!"

When Ralph has been out late at a chess tournament, I can tell, when he crawls into bed, whether he won or lost by the low, almost imperceptible sigh that bespeaks failure. And Ralph can tell what kind of day I've had by the way I plunk the main course down on the supper table as though daring anybody to ask what's in it.

The trick, of course, is to put these clues to work —to use them as signs of a person's needing love or reassurance or sympathy or support. If we merely exist side by side with our families, ignoring the little peculiarities, we might as well be roomers in a large boardinghouse, separate from each other.

That's what makes a family different, what makes it special. Jack might have been annoyed if he knew I'd read the note I found in his jeans' pocket before washing them: "Dear Jack, please don't forget to bring me a picture of yourself on Monday like you promised. Love, Marcia."

But I'll bet he was glad, when Monday came and he started to bound out the door empty-handed, that I said, "This is Monday, Jack. Think! Is there *anything* at all you're supposed to take to school?"

With a look of gratitude and relief, he rushed back up to his room, stuffed something into his pocket, and was off again. I could have cautioned him not to sit on it all day, but that would have been going too far.

Detectives may follow a case through to its conclusion, but a mother knows when to bug out.

111]

THE THANKFUL BOX

No matter where we lived when I was a child, we always had an attic. And in that attic was a big black trunk which Mother called the "Keepsake Chest." It wasn't filled entirely with treasures. In the winter it contained swimsuits and sandals and in the summer it held our wool sweaters, but underneath these seasonal garments was a wealth of "keepsakes" that only we could appreciate. Once or twice each year, on some impossible day when the rain was pelting down or the snow building up and all us children whined about boredom, Mother would mention the Keepsake Chest, and we would trek to the attic to take out all our assorted treasures one by one.

There was a pair of little wooden shoes that an uncle had bought for my mother in Holland; there were two Russian dolls, origin unknown, which had lost their hair; there was a gingham dress with long waist and ruffles that my mother had worn back in 1904, and a pink silk dress that I had worn when I was small. There was a little straw donkey from Mexico and some old quartet music belonging to my father, old photographs, and a tintype of a great-great-grandmother who looked as though she were capable of driving a team of horses through Nebraska single-handed. There was a box of baby teeth and some once-loved teddy bears, clay bowls we had made in school, report cards, drawings, poems, books, and posters. There were letters of congratulations and letters of condolence, certificates of accomplishment and perfect attendance pins.

Each item was held up for all to see. Each was exclaimed over in turn. Each deserved its own little story before it was lovingly put back in its place once more. And if the house had ever caught fire, we would all have rushed to save the Keepsake Chest. It was sweet, sad, and utterly mundane, but us nonetheless.

I'm starting a Keepsake Chest of our own, only we call it our Thankful Box. It is slowly being filled with bits and pieces of ourselves—reminders of things we have done, places we have been. It's a box of treasures that says we belong to each other and to this family, that we are thankful we can share them with each other, and that they mean something to us, even if the junkman wouldn't give us a nickel for the whole batch.

ON NESTING IN THE
NUCLEAR AGE

Given our day and age, I marvel that we are not all psychotic. With world-spending for armaments almost $1 million per minute, I wonder that we even bother to get out of bed in the mornings.

It used to be that death was an individual thing or a catastrophe of limited proportions. When we died, we consoled ourselves, there would be relatives left to mourn us, to bury us, to remember . . . Our favorite books and keepsakes would be passed on to our grandchildren, and the great monuments—the Parthenon, the Pantheon, the Sistine Chapel—would remain as tributes to man's creativity and genius.

There is no longer that assurance. I have held off telling my children about The Bomb as long as I can. Only when they ask do I answer.

"You know what Gary said?" Jack related recently. "That a hydrogen bomb could destroy a whole city."

I felt an old familiar flash of panic. So it was to be Jack's turn.

"Yes," I said. "That's true."

He waited, hoping for a qualifying statement that never came.

"And everybody in it?"

"Yes, pretty much so, I'm afraid."

He watched my face. "Wouldn't there be any place to hide?"

I thought of the people trapped in bomb shelters with infernos raging above them over the air vents, of people emerging from bomb shelters to find that they and all possible food supplies had been contaminated. I thought of the absence of hospitals, doctors, and pain killers. I thought of the islands of the North Pacific—the site of nuclear tests twenty years ago—and how the government has now declared some of them unsafe for thousands of years to come.

"Not really," I said, and when he crumbled, I held him close.

But I do not believe in leaving my children without hope. I told Jack that the awfulness of the weapons should, in itself, be a deterrent against using them; I told him what Margaret Mead said about the longer the human race goes without a nuclear war, the better the chance that we can avoid one altogether; I told him that since nuclear power was discovered, many situations have been resolved by negotiation that might formerly have ended in war.

Then I gave him my pep talk about how sudden death is always a possibility, even without nuclear weapons. I explained that people have always faced the threat of war, and whole villages must have trembled at the approach of a Viking ship. I told him how many peace organizations there are. I squeezed every drop of hope that I could from the reaches of my soul and ended, at last, by telling him that it is not how long we live, but how well, whether it be a hundred years, forty, or a mere ten.

Jack found his particular solace.

"Well," he said finally, releasing his arms from around my neck, "at least if the bomb ever falls, we'll all die together."

I let him go with that. I did not tell him that he might be at school and Ralph at the office and Peter and Susan who knows where. We need all the hope we can get.

How do parents stay sane, however, with a constant awareness of the unthinkable? This parent remains in a semi-conscious state by a roundabout reasoning that goes as follows:

> It is at least possible that there will be no nuclear war. It is also possible that I could spend my life worrying about a holocaust only to lose my children under the wheels of a school bus.

That is known as stage one. Sometimes it helps and sometimes it doesn't. If it doesn't, I resort to emergency logic:

> Even if our children have only a few more years to live, I want them to have the happiest, most productive life possible, because it's the only life they're going to get. I must help our chil-

dren live *as if* they will reach old age. They must be given responsibility, respect, and love in abundance, and they must have hope.

This is why we plan for college, for retirement, for grandchildren. When I'm ninety and toothless, I want to gather my great-grandchildren about me and, in a quavery croon, tell them how when the world was young and nations were stupid we almost blew ourselves to kingdom come. And I hope that things will have changed so much by then that my descendants will yawn, exchange amused glances, and chalk it off as another one of the old girl's stories.

COUNTING OUR BLESSINGS

Gramps is as unique a personality as ever existed, but we don't always see eye to eye on how to raise children. When Ralph and I were small, all that parents worried about was keeping their children alive until they reached eighteen. Today, in this permissive age, Gramps sees Susan spend more for a coat then he earned in a whole week back in 1932. And as for a Thanksgiving table laden with sweet potatoes and gravy and mints and pies and ice cream, he wonders if anyone remembers when he sold apples at the corner of State and Madison on Saturday afternoons.

Nonetheless, having Gramps at the head of the table on Thanksgiving is as traditional as the turkey itself, and this particular year he arrived as usual in his 1962 Ford with his red vest and gold tie, and dinner began on schedule with a poem that Peter had composed at school.

It was not, however, a poem about thankfulness, the title being "Save the Last Piece for Me." The children were not in one of their better moods. I had promised Jack and Peter the drumsticks, thinking Susan too old to care, and she came to the table sulking and said she didn't want any of the dumb old bird at all.

Jack, meanwhile, declared that the chestnuts in the dressing ruined it, and when Peter looked over at the sideboard and discovered I'd made only mince pies this year and no pumpkin, he said it was a stupid Thanksgiving dinner.

Up until now, Gramps had borne it all silently. Up until now he had listened without comment to the griping from both sides of the table. But suddenly, at Peter's remark, he stood up, picked up the turkey platter in one hand and the sweet potatoes in the other, and said, "Well, if nobody's aware of the starving children in India, I'll just remove this turkey from the table." And he did. Before the children could close their astonished mouths, he was back for the cranberries and gravy. "And if nobody's grateful for the bounteous blessings which God has bestowed on us, I'll remove these, too," he said, and disappeared.

At this point I would have settled for a simple thank-you to the cook, but now the children were being grateful all over the place. Gramps made each of them recite five reasons why sitting at our Thanksgiving table was preferable to sitting on a sidewalk in Calcutta before he brought back the turkey. It was probably the most appreciated dinner I've ever made.

ON GENEROSITY

Our children do not get presents except on special occasions. We have never made it a practice to buy them something every time we go shopping. Consequently, at Christmas they can each expect several modest gifts.

Once a Depression girl, however, always a Depression girl, and as I wrap the children's gifts, I cannot help but remember how little I received each Christmas when I was their ages. The most marvelous present I ever got was an entire outfit for my doll from leftover sewing scraps. I thought I was the luckiest girl in the world.

Consequently, when Susan told me not to give her a skirt this year because she wouldn't wear it, I felt my hackles rising. When Jack presented me with a list of things he couldn't live without, I felt down-right indignant. But leave it to Peter to be direct.

"How many presents am I getting this year, Mommy?" he chirped over waffles at breakfast.

Now Peter, being the youngest, deserves patience.

"I'm sure you will get quite enough," I told him, "but you know, Christmas is a time to think of other people, to decide what you will give to everyone else."

"Oh, that's all taken care of," he said simply. "I made 'em out of clay at school and wrapped 'em in Kleenex."

"Still," I went on, "we give gifts to others to show our love. Do you understand?"

Peter nodded and went on tracing airplanes in his syrup, and I thought the matter settled.

It unnerved me, therefore, when Peter came to me the following day and said, "How many gifts am I getting this year, Mommy?"

What does it take, anyway, to instill a little altruism in a child? What does a parent have to do to promote generosity and good will? I put on my most tragic face and turned sad eyes in his direction.

"Peter," I said, "don't you remember what we

were talking about yesterday? Christmas is a time to think about *giving,* not *getting.*"

Peter stared at me thoughtfully, and I felt that deep in his eyes, somewhere down in his heart of hearts, the message had finally gotten through.

"All right," he said brightly, "how many presents are you *giving* me, then?"

THE DISCARDS

Every December I clean out the basement, partly to see how many discarded toys there may be from Christmases past. This serves as a reminder never to buy (1) a battery-operated game; (2) a toy that makes noise; (3) anything which promises that one's father can assemble it in less than one afternoon. (So why is it that each December, the only gift in the world that Peter wants is battery operated, incredibly loud, and takes two and a half days to assemble?)

In any case, the first week of December finds me attacking every corner with broom and wastebasket, mad to throw away anything that doesn't have a utilitarian value.

I move ruthlessly from one end to another like a human bulldozer, and the heap of junk overflows into boxes and sacks: sheets of cardboard; Styrofoam packing; clay which has inexplicably been rolled in sand; rubber gloves with a rip down one side; old shirts; empty coffee cans; boards with nails stuck in them; string with knots in it; empty milk cartons; and cinder block which has broken into a number of assorted pieces. All these things have been used on and off all year by Peter and Jack to make Frankenstein's castle, coal mines, roller coasters, and such.

I carry my bounty to the trash cans with glee. I laugh as the garbage truck hauls it away. I go down into the basement again and again to admire the wide open spaces.

It's only a matter of days before Peter says, "We're going to paint next week in art class, and I have to bring an old shirt and an empty milk carton."

It is only a matter of weeks before Jack says, "What happened to those pieces of Styrofoam in the basement, Mom? I have to make a science exhibit."

It is only a matter of time before Susan discovers she had a use for the rubber gloves, Ralph for the coffee cans, and me for pieces of cinder block.

This year, as I approach the basement once more, I hold each unwanted item in my hand and try to picture all possible uses for it. If my imagination comes up with nothing, it goes into the trash can as usual, but you can bet that by January 1, I'll wish it was ours once more.

TRADITION

I've often looked wistfully at old-fashioned scenes on Christmas cards and wished that our family had some holiday traditions. Why couldn't we go into the forest looking for yule logs? I wondered. Why couldn't we bundle up in red and green scarves and go caroling? Why couldn't we have candlelight processions up and down the staircase, roast a pig with an apple in its mouth, or present a Christmas pageant to admiring relatives? Tradition, that's what I want—big healthy chunks of it to remember when I'm old and gray.

As I was baking my usual Swedish almond cookies this year, however, I heard the children talking in the next room.

"This is the part of Christmas I like best," Susan was saying, "when Mom makes all the cookies and the house smells good for days. She always does the almond cookies first, then the chocolate curls, and then the lemon bars."

Do I? I wondered. You mean there's a pattern to my holiday baking that the children detected and enjoyed?

"I like mailing the packages," Peter commented. "And putting on the seals."

Mailing packages? I choked. That was a tradition? Well, sort of. Since our relatives are scattered all over the United States, there comes a week early in December when the gifts are wrapped, packed in boxes, decorated with seals, and carted off in the back of the station wagon to the post office.

"You've got to be kidding," said Jack. "Nothing is better than Christmas Eve."

"Yeah," said Susan, "we always build a fire and sit around looking at the old picture albums."

"And Mom puts a plate of fudge on the table," added Peter.

"And we turn out all the lights except the Christmas tree and look at the shadows," said Jack.

"And call Gramps," said Peter.

Glory be, we do have traditions! I thought. We're creating them each time we repeat something that's fun and meaningful to the whole family. Never mind that it's a pilgrimage to the post office instead of the forest; never mind that fudge takes the place of wassail or that photo albums entertain us in place of a candlelight procession.

Tradition creeps up on us when we least suspect it, and I rather imagine I'll have lots to remember when I'm old and gray.

FIVE

Life on the Outside

WHEN THE FBI DROPPED IN

I didn't realize my own importance. I didn't even know they cared.

It all began with the *Washington Post* and an article on the Freedom of Information Act. Anyone, it said, could request a look at his FBI file. *Why not?* said a small voice with more *chutzpah* than sense. What about all those protest marches? What about that picketing of the White House? In fact, if they *didn't* have a file on me, could my ego take it?

I wrote to the FBI. Ralph, watching from the sidelines, commented dryly that if I wasn't on a list before, I would be now. Two months later I was informed that there was a file for a person of my name, but it would take a notarized signature to release it. I was also advised that I was #56,275. At least I had company. I sent a notarized signature.

At this point I began to take the matter seriously. What had started out as a lark became an exercise in logic. How had they gotten my name? How, among all those thousands of people at the reflecting pool when Martin Luther King gave his oration, had they singled out any of us? How had they identified any of those who held silent vigils outside the White House during the napalming of Vietnam?

In due course a manila folder arrived at our house. It contained no references to either peace or civil rights activities. The FBI forgave all that. Instead, they were investigating my relationship with a man I'd never seen.

A few years back, it seems, I wrote a letter to my senator protesting the arrest of a Korean poet, Kim Chi Ha. He was imprisoned, if I remember, because he wrote a poem against the South Korean regime. And because I am allergic to the persecution of poets, I wanted to express my outrage. I did not think my gesture would win Kim Chi Ha his release, but I have this thing about freedom.

My senator dutifully passed along my letter to the State Department and sent a copy of their reply to me. They confirmed that Kim Chi Ha had been imprisoned because he had "violated Korea's broadly worded anti-Communist laws" and stated that "the Department fully understands the concern which your constituent has expressed for the welfare of this young poet."

They lied. If they had fully understood my concern, they would not have sent my letter to the FBI. The FBI understood even less and promptly checked the criminal records of three local police jurisdictions, the Civil Service Commission, and the Park Police. (What kind of mayhem would I be committing in a park, I wonder?) According to the once-confidential file, they sent "special agent F-202" out to the house to check out my car and made a "no-name telephonic inquiry."

I remember the phone call well. The man said he was putting together a list for jury duty, and wondered why I used different versions of my name. I explained how it was with writers and thought that was the end of it. Strange that I was never called for jury duty. Stranger still was agent F-202's report, which made no mention of my occupation:

> . . . through a no-name telephonic inquiry, Phyllis Naylor volunteered that . . . she will use either Phyllis Reynolds Naylor or Phyllis Dean Naylor, depending on the circumstances, thereby allowing her the opportunity to use her maiden name . . . During the above-mentioned no-name inquiry, Naylor volunteered the information that she is self-employed and works out of her own home.

Sinister, yes? Dynamite in the basement, perhaps? This is what Hollywood plots are made of. Should I option off the rights?

The dropping in of the FBI to check out the car did cause a brief flurry of excitement in our house. We wondered whether they actually managed to get in it. Jack said they have special keys, and there's a hole in the floor that Peter insists they crawled through. Susan was content to brag that hers was the only mother on the block with an FBI record, but they've forgotten all that now.

Not I, however. Not quite. According to the records, all documents are not yet in. Someone, somewhere, is still working away on the Naylor file at the taxpayer's expense, and the weather's getting cold. Every so often I imagine something moving out behind the azalea bushes. Come in, come in, Agent F-202, wherever you are. I'll confess all over a cup of hot coffee.

THE TRASH TRIBULATION

There are people about who need, but can't afford, a pair of shoes or a winter coat or a washing machine. There are also people about who, despite the inflation that is eating us up, have these things to give away. The trick is to get the two together, and that surely shouldn't be too difficult. Not so. Here in Maryland the local charitable organizations are three weeks behind in their pickup of unwanted items, and you can't find someone to steal that old pair of shoes, much less the used washing machine.

Every county has its laws about what you can and cannot put out for the garbage truck, and what people do with such items is a story of courage and ingenuity, not to mention fraud.

If the police try to get me to testify, I'll plead the Fifth, but I know a woman who got rid of her son's rock collection (fist-sized rocks from every state in the Union) by dropping them in a dozen empty milk containers and distributing them here and there among the garbage. I have a neighbor who filled three grocery bags halfway with leftover shingles and the rest of the way with coffee grounds and orange peel. And a desperate owner of four oak trees finally got rid of his leaves by dragging them into the house by the bushel and burning them in the fireplace.

There is even a scurrilous person somewhere in the area who sneaks around at night after the trash cans are out and distributes his uncollectables—an automobile seat here, some bathroom tile there—beside random cans. When the trash men come and go and the seat and tile remain untouched, they have then become the uncollectables of somebody else.

The problem, of course, is guilt. No one feels right about replacing a perfectly good refrigerator for a newer model unless he is sure that the old one is being put to good use. And he doesn't want the old refrigerator teetering on the edge of the curb until Goodwill decides to pick it up. He particularly doesn't want the Goodwill driver to take one look at it and reject it even for the poverty pockets.

Something like this happened to a friend. The woman was so distraught that she stayed out on the driveway all night dismantling her old oven piece by

131]

piece, wrapped each piece in newspaper tied with string, and deposited a parcel a week in her garbage can, until the oven was gone.

I don't know whether we Americans are buying too much too fast, or whether the things we buy just don't hold up. But it wouldn't surprise me if purgatory consists of having to write out the model, make, and serial number of every appliance and contraption that isn't allowed to live out its natural life span with its original owner.

SAGA OF THE BROWN, GREEN, AND PURPLE

The place to make a horrible confession is not, I know, in print. I thought of writing it down on a scrap of paper and slipping it to the art teacher inside an apple. I considered sending an anonymous letter to the superintendent or even picketing the school with a paper bag over my head.

But somewhere there must be other souls who want to protect the T-shirt and who share my unspoken aversion to those wet monstrosities children lug home from school called tie-dyed-anything-you-happen-to-have-handy.

Now I have accepted clay bowls with praise and delight. I have hung papier-mâché kangaroos from light fixtures and decorated refrigerator doors with untold finger paintings. But tie-dying is something else. For those of you who haven't had a child in school for the past ten years, it is a process whereby, according to my six-year-old, "You take this T-shirt, see, and you tie knots in it, and then you 'sklunk' it in this big pot of red stuff and then the blue stuff and then the green stuff, and that's how I got my pants all dirty."

I've been through it before, of course, with Jack, who is in fifth grade. Innocently I sent him off to the dye pot with a new white T-shirt, pillowcase, and a pair of summer shorts. I didn't recognize them when he brought them back. The shirt was a strange color I had never seen before, best described as brown-green-purple. There was an orange splotch on one shoulder and a streak of yellow down the back. It looked like the dog's breakfast, but the pillowcase and shorts were even worse. And when they were washed—well, it's too awful even to talk about.

I thought instantly of the Salvation Army, Goodwill, and the Disabled American Veterans. But my son actually wanted to wear that shirt. He wanted to race up and down the street with all the other tie-dyed boys and girls, drying in the early spring sunshine.

Since that day, other mothers have whispered their awful secrets to me. One collects all her child's disintegrating underwear and sends them off for the dyeing. Another slyly chooses only the clothes her daughter has outgrown, and still another, in desperation, once sent the empty laundry bag.

The problem is that children adore seeing their pure white apparel ruined before their very eyes, and tie-dyeing is awaited with great anticipation. Therefore, do you think it would be too disrespectful to suggest that after the assembled items have been "sklunked" and dunked at will, the art teacher take them all home as cherished evidence of the creativity of childhood?

PROHIBITION

I know all about the children of Israel—the plagues and persecution—the whole bit. But there are times I envy that manna from heaven, be it ever so humble or bland or boring.

Back in the days when I was growing up, there was no question as to what we would take in our lunch boxes. By the time we'd walked a mile and a half to school, we'd settle for anything at all between two slices of bread. It might be leftover roast from the night before, or a piece of thick bologna.

It might be a cold fried egg or a slab of cheese. It could be hamburger, fried chicken, sliced pork, or homemade jelly. There was hot soup in a thermos, an apple or orange, and a big piece of pie for dessert. Lunch was a real occasion, and we ate slowly, enjoying the mingled aroma of peanut butter, baked ham, and cherry pie.

It's not as simple any more. No mother concerned about nitrites is going to give her children bologna, salami, ham, or bacon. If she's worried about cholesterol, she'll go easy on eggs, and, of course, everyone's talking about the connection between red meat and cancer.

How many days can a child eat chicken without beginning to squawk? How many days can he eat peanut butter or cheese without his tongue being permanently stuck to the roof of his mouth?

Susan says she's the only one in her class who takes strawberry yogurt instead of a sandwich in her lunch sack. Jack insists that nobody, absolutely nobody, carries celery and carrots wrapped in cellophane, and Peter wants to know why he can't have cream-filled, coconut-coated, chocolate cupcakes, two to a package, like all the other kids.

And what do you do for a breath of fresh air nowadays? Do you risk sending the children outdoors to play, or do you keep them in where the air is filtered? Do you keep them in the shade and deprive them of Vitamin D, or do you send them out in the sun and risk skin cancer? Should they drink water from the faucet, or should you buy it bottled?

Life, it occurs to me, was very simple before the advent of all these precautions. Do they really have any effect? If I go without bacon for the rest of my natural life, will I really live an extra ten years, or is this cruel and unusual punishment?

I don't know. I hate to think of the prohibitions that will be in force when *my* children are parents. But one thing's sure: when I reach my ninetieth birthday, I'm going to sit myself down to a steak with gravy, oodles of butter, and a whipped cream pie, and if I expire right then and there, at least I'll go happily.

A SCHOLASTIC SCHISM

Somebody should make me superintendent of schools for a week and I'd make some curriculum changes you wouldn't believe. For one thing, I would have math problems that resembled real life: instead of counting how many pencils in five gross (did you ever buy a gross of anything?), I would have kids figuring out how many Good Humor bars it would cost them if they had just broken a garage window and would have to forfeit their allowance of forty-five cents for twenty-one weeks. Instead of memorizing the layers of the earth's crust, I would have them memorize the numbers of all the interstate highways within a fifty-mile radius. And rather than have them study sentence structure, I would give them a course in communication, which would emphasize speaking without profanity, listening without interruption, and developing the ability to reflect upon the other person's point of view.

I would make sure that no kid graduated from high school until he had learned to change a light bulb and replace a fuse. I'd make a diploma conditional upon learning to run all three cycles on the washing machine and finding the serial number on the dryer. Students of the Naylor System would have to know that Bach was a composer, not a candy manufacturer, and that Renoir was not the trade name for a hair spray.

My students would have to know how to buy a plane ticket and switch flights in Denver. They'd have to be able to use their own two legs to walk to the library and do something more in the kitchen than defrost pizza and a little Sara Lee. There would be field trips to the hospital emergency rooms to see what somebody looks like after a motorcycle accident, and they'd learn to bend, fold, and mutilate computer payment cards when the bill was wrong and they couldn't get anyone's attention.

I don't know if my school would be accredited. I don't know if my students would ever make it to college. But I'll bet there wouldn't be a single one of them jumping out of a ten-story window when he was forty years old because he couldn't cope.

SAFETY VALVE

Returning from church last Sunday, Peter confided that he sometimes has this terrible fear he might jump off the balcony during the service and land in the lap of some startled lady below.

I know what he means. When I was young, sitting stone-still beside my mother, resisting the urge to scratch, or kick my legs, or lick all the offertory envelopes on the back of the pew in front, I sometimes had the awful thought that I might rise from my seat, give a blood-curdling yell, and go cartwheeling down the aisle to the altar.

It was not just a vagrant thought. It was a recurring nightmare that kept me glued to my seat, made me grip the edge of the pew in a deathlock, and forced me always to take an inside seat so that, should my id get the upper hand, my mother could grab me before it was too late.

The fantasy absorbed me. I would imagine the startled pause of the minister as I gave my war whoop; I could see the stares of the women as I rose from my seat; I felt the horror of the entire congregation as I cartwheeled down to the altar.

Finally, I confided it all to my mother. She said that it was nature's way of working off a small girl's tension during a long sermon, and that fantasizing helped insure that it would never really come about. But if it should, she said, the preacher would understand.

Somehow the fear dissipated. Somehow the thought that a calm, understanding face would meet my yelling and acrobatics took the zest out of the whole idea. And that's why I told Peter that if he ever jumped off the balcony and landed in a lady's lap, we would understand.

He stared at me a full half-minute before he slumped down in the back seat and turned his attention to the window.

"It was a lousy idea," he muttered. But he's sure to think up a replacement.

ANTICIPATING PAIN

When Susan began junior high school, she came home to report that some day soon there would be a

"Seventh-Grade Sing Day." Then she went up to her room and bawled.

We finally got to the facts: all seventh-graders were supposedly taught the school song at a pep rally. The junior-high basketball team hoped that all the new students would show up for the first game, cheering madly and singing with gusto, and it was to this end that Seventh-Grade Sing Day had come into being. On this day it was the privilege of any eighth- or ninth-grader to stop new students in the hall and demand that they sing the school song. All sorts of punishments and humiliations were supposedly in store for those who did not comply—as though being backed up against the wall and asked to sing solo was not humiliation enough.

What do I do? I wondered, and knew, as soon as I'd asked, that the answer was *nothing.* Much as a mama might like, she does not go to the principal and demand that the tradition be stopped. She does not follow her daughter around school on the appointed day to help ward off evil. And she does not give in to the cowardly impulse to keep her daughter home.

I remember my freshman year of high school. It was torturous not because of what happened, which was nothing, but because of what we expected. We had been told that some time during our freshman year, all the senior boys would storm the girls' locker room during gym and steal whatever they could find —a wholesale panty raid. Of course, it never happened, and never had, but for an entire year we girls would rush to the showers like lemmings to the sea, clutching our towels around us and praying we could get there and back, before the seniors arrived.

There was little I could do for Susan except treat the whole thing lightly and urge her to do the same. With Susan, however, this was impossible. Every night she would go to her room and practice the song over and over. Each morning she would set out, books in her arms, resignation on her face, and I would ache for the hurt she was feeling. The big day was set only to be postponed. The worst was always yet to come.

And finally, one day, it happened. One day when I was busy with other things and had forgotten to ache, Susan burst in, collapsed on the sofa, and said, "It's over!"

You would have thought she'd just had her tonsils out or climbed a mountain, at least. I sank down gratefully beside her to hear all the gory details.

It's unfair, you know. Each of my kids has to go through it only once: I've got to experience it again with Jack and Peter.

GOING INCOGNITO

There are times that I wish it were Halloween all year long. It's not so much that I wish the kids would go around in masks, but that I wish *I* had a mask. There are times when I would like to be disassociated from my family—when I would like to look at them disinterestedly, as one looks at strangers or, better yet, ignore them completely.

When we go out to dinner and Peter hunches over his plate shoving monstrous bites of food into his mouth, I would like very much to hang a sign on him that says, "This is a starving child from abroad whom we are befriending."

When I am entertaining members of my guild and Jack comes crashing into the kitchen, bangs a cupboard door, and belches loudly, I want to be able to say, "Excuse me, but I think the neighbor's child has wandered in again."

When Susan and I are shopping and she breaks into tears in front of a sales clerk because the jeans she wants don't fit, I want to whisper to the clerk that she is an emotionally disturbed niece who is visiting for the weekend.

Don't think that my fantasies stop with the kids, either. There are times, when Ralph forgets the name of a person I introduced him to only a week before, that I have this tremendous urge to keep right on walking and pretend I don't know him.

Of course, it works both ways. When, descending the staircase of a rather grand hotel, I accidentally dropped my handbag over the railing, spewing cosmetics, subway tokens, and cough drops in fifty-seven directions, my family must have wished they could carry me out the service entrance.

But that's the way it is with families. The best and the worst part is that they are ours, forever and ever, and who, really, would want to change that?

ON CENSORS

I was thinking the other day about books I once loved and stopped by the library to pick up a copy of *Little Black Sambo*.

"Good heavens, that book has been banned for five years," the librarian told me.

Banned, did she say? That marvelous little black boy who was almost eaten alive in the jungle?

143]

"Yes," the librarian said, "because of his purple shoes with crimson soles and crimson linings."

"What?" I screeched.

"Some people think," she said, "that the portrayal of a black family as liking bright colors demeans them somehow, so we took it off the shelf."

I was saddened to hear it. I love purple and crimson myself.

"Do you have *Albert's Toothache,* then?" I asked, remembering the book that Peter had requested.

The librarian looked embarrassed. "There's been so much controversy about that one, we're withholding it for the present," she told me.

"Albert's a turtle," I said. "He can love any color he likes without offending anybody."

"Yes, but Albert's mother was wearing an apron throughout the book, and some people decided that this was demeaning to women."

I learned a lot that day. I learned that if all the groups who want books censored or slanted get control of our libraries, there aren't going to be any children's books at all. Homosexual groups want loving male and female couples portrayed; feminist groups go bananas unless the mother in the story is working; religious groups want more references to God; atheist groups want less of it; and just recently a psychologist compiled a list of all books dealing with death and requested that the library get rid of them.

I can agree to a point. If *every* book, or *most*

books, portrayed blacks as natives walking through jungles in purple shoes or women as mindless robots tending the kichen, we should object. But if every book from here on in is going to be censored, and only idealized plots can ever get through, what kind of reality is it that we present to our children?

I have enough faith in our writers and publishers and librarians and the reading public in general to believe that a large variety of books reach our children and that they can select or reject books as their parents are allowed to do. And if Little Black Sambo prefers crimson to burnt sienna and Albert's mother likes to putter about the stove, I say it's nobody's business but their own.

DINNER GUESTS

Peter was unusually interested in Thanksgiving this year. For the first time in his short life he was beginning to understand the connection between turkey and the Thanksgiving feast, and he suddenly got it in his head that we should invite an Indian.

"If there were any around, I'd be glad to," I told him, absorbed in my shopping list.

Peter surveyed me for a moment. "Well, if I find

one, can I ask him home to dinner?"

"Sure," I said blithely. "You can invite the whole tribe."

That was the Monday before Thanksgiving. On Tuesday Peter told me he was still looking. On Wednesday he said he might have found an Indian, but he wasn't sure. And on Thanksgiving morning, just as I was putting the pies in the oven, the phone rang, and a woman said that Peter had invited her son and the family to dinner at two, and she wondered if I was expecting them.

For a moment my brain went haywire computing the pieces of pie, the slices of turkey, the servings of sweet potatoes, and I wondered if we all ate a little less . . .

"Of course we are," I said. "I'm just not sure how many are coming."

"Six," she said.

"Marvelous," I replied, feeling faint. "We'd love to have you."

When I hung up, I pounced on Peter so quickly that I took his breath away. "Why didn't you tell me you had invited a whole family?" I gasped.

"I wasn't sure they could come," he croaked.

"Who are they?"

"I don't know their last name."

"Where do they live?"

He didn't know that, either.

"This dinner," I said to Ralph, "is going to be one heck of a surprise."

It turned out that the Shapiri family had moved into our neighborhood five months before from India, the father being with the diplomatic corps. The parents spoke fluent English and the four children were learning it at school. They were fascinated by the Thanksgiving tradition and appreciated being invited.

That evening, I tactfully explained to Peter the difference between American Indians and the Indians of the East.

"Does it really matter?" Peter asked, somewhat chagrined.

"Not a bit," I said, honestly. "Wasn't it a marvelous day?"

PROGRESSIVE SPEECH

If, as a child, I did something bizarre, like walking about the house leaving a trail of salt in my wake, I was told instantly to stop and clean it up. Nobody thought to ask me why I was sprinkling the rugs with salt, and it's just as well, since I didn't know. It just seemed like a good idea at the time.

Today, however, we parents know that there are things one must say to one's children. "Why" takes precedence over everything else:

Why did you bite your sister?

Why do you wear your shirts backwards?

Why are you stuffing that green bean through the crack in the table?

We are warned against such phrases as "When I was your age," "What will the neighbors think?" and "Wait till your father gets home." And we certainly must remember, when a child comes home from school with an artistic creation, to say, "Tell me about your picture," not "What is it?" or "What on earth is it?" which is even worse.

Yesterday I remembered with Peter.

"Guess," he said.

There were tiny puffs of white cotton pasted here and there on the picture, so I said, "I'll bet it has something to do with winter."

"Right."

I looked at the strange creatures on the paper. They obviously had significance for Peter, but all I could think of were the horses in Revelation, issuing fire, smoke, and sulphur from their nostrils.

"Lions?" I said. "Wintertime at the zoo?"

"Nope," said Peter.

I studied it some more. Then I noticed that the objects, whatever they were, were flying.

"*Star Wars?*" I offered. "*Star Wars* in winter?"

A head emerged from behind the picture. Peter looked at it himself to make sure.

"Uh uh," he said.

"Locusts?" I bleated. "One of the plagues?"

Two eyes peered at me from over the picture.

"No," said a disgusted voice.

"You know, I was never very good at guessing, Peter," I said. "Why don't you just tell me?"

"Santa Claus's reindeer," said Peter.

Can you imagine what I did to his spontaneity, not to mention his morale? It's not fair, you know. If we parents can learn to say, "Tell me about your picture," children can be taught to say something besides "Guess."

PANIC

Having lived in Chicago, Minneapolis, and on a farm in Iowa, I was not quite prepared for what I found when I moved east. In Iowa, for example, we walked a mile to school each day, and if the snowdrifts were over our heads, we simply started out fifteen minutes earlier than usual. In Chicago, when the wind cut through us like icy stilettos, we automatically wore double layers of clothes to work. In Minneapolis, where there was a foot of snow on the ground from December to March, we often went to the store pulling sleds.

Maryland, however, is a different story. Perhaps it

is our proximity to Washington that makes us so crisis-oriented we'll overreact to anything. If I must be caught in a snowstorm in the dead of winter, let it be in Montana or Vermont or Alaska; anywhere but here.

All you need is a half-inch of snow on the major streets and you've got the worst pileup you ever saw. Cars skid sideways, causing a backup for three miles. Volkswagens veer off into ditches, buses plow into embankments, and traffic in downtown Washington is completely immobile for a radius of nine blocks.

Let the first snowflake fall on a winter afternoon, and all phone lines to the schools are jammed. Let the fiftieth or sixtieth snowflake fall, and schools are closed early. If one wakes up in the morning to find that snow has fallen during the night, radios blare out the news that all schools will open an hour and a half late, but if you fail to keep listening and pack your child off at ten-thirty instead of nine, you may discover that a further announcement closed the schools for the entire day.

Schools are nothing compared to the supermarkets, however. I heard that once, years ago, the side effects of Hurricane Hazel caused so much havoc that some of the roads were flooded, and a few householders in outlying areas could not make it in to town for a week. So now, at the first hint of trouble, stores are jammed to capacity, and housewives whose freezers and cupboards already hold a six-month supply go skidding and sliding along the roads to buy a side of beef before the storm gets worse, only to discover that if they'd waited a day, the sun would have melted the snow and the roads would have been dry.

The Second Coming is too long to wait. Christ ought to come back now for a preview, sit on the steps of the Capitol, and repeat his Sermon on the Mount to this frantic, frenetic metropolis. Of course, it would never work: somebody would note that he wasn't wearing shoes and haul him off as a protester, but he ought to give it a go. If a real crisis ever came to Washington, I'd want us to have something more to fall back on than snow tires and a side of beef.

A FUNCTIONAL DISORDER

Gramps has rarely been to our house for Christmas because he prefers the warm sun of Florida to the unpredictable snowstorms of a Maryland December.

Each year I send him a big box of presents and homemade cookies, with pictures and notes from the children. But Christmas never seems complete unless we hear his voice, and it's become as much a tradition to call Gramps on Christmas Eve as it is to

151]

hang up Peter's stocking.

But it's more than a tradition. It's an obstacle course, a full-fledged endurance test. With everyone's parents in Florida these days, and all families in all fifty states trying to call them at once, it's like Bedlam and the Tower of Babel and The Bell System all rolled up into one.

This year was the worst. No sooner had I dialed his area code than the phone went berserk. It started to ring, then switched to busy, then clicked and buzzed a few times, and finally I heard an operator in Kansas say that she had completed my call to Los Angeles. I pressed the button to break the connection and released it.

"Hello," came a voice.

"Merry Christmas," I said wonderingly.

"Gee, it's good to hear from you, honey. I'm amazed you got through."

I was a little amazed myself, especially since I knew it wasn't Gramps. There was a pause.

"Is this Elizabeth?" the stranger asked.

"No, I'm afraid the connections are crossed," I told him. "I'm Phyllis Naylor, from Maryland."

"How about that! I'm Ed Farmer from Cedar Falls, Iowa, waiting for a call from my daughter. How's the weather out there in Maryland?"

"Two inches of snow last night," I told him. "The kids are delighted."

"That's a good Christmas present," he said. "You should have seen the storm that blew in here last week! If you ever want to see a really white Christmas, you should come to Cedar Falls."

"Maybe we will," I said.

It was almost nine-thirty when we got through to Gramps, and I wondered if he'd been lonely, waiting for our call on Christmas Eve. But he'd had a marvelous time. Whenever he picked up the receiver, he discovered someone was waiting to get through to someone somewhere, and so far he'd talked with a woman from New York, a rancher in Nevada, and a small boy from Wisconsin who was calling his own grandfather and never knew the difference.

NOEL

I have heard it said that things done on the spur of the moment often turn out surprisingly well. Possibly. One night, however, some friends came over for dinner; after dinner we sang carols, and—giddy, perhaps, from the wassail—we decided we sounded simply great and would treat the whole neighborhood.

We bundled up in boots and scarves, brought along a pitch pipe, and headed for the house at the end of the street.

I don't know how they did it in the olden days. Maybe they warned everyone that they were coming. Maybe they put an announcement in the town square. I guess that was our mistake. No one could tell us from the local sanitation department.

When we finally got up the sixteen steps to the house on the hill, gathered under the picture window, found our note, and began "The First Noel," something entirely unexpected happened. The lights went out. It was as though we had blown a fuse. We were debating whether to stop or go on to the second verse when we saw faces peering out at us through slats in the Venetian blind. And when, at the end of the second verse, the house remained dark, we decided that the people preferred us to leave. We went next door.

This time we had no sooner begun "Oh Come All Ye Faithful" than the family came crowding out, insisted we take a handful of pennies and nickels, and disappeared back inside, closing the door behind them.

At the third house, someone opened a window and asked us please to come back some other time because they were watching their favorite TV program, and at the last house, a woman asked if we were collecting just clothes or would we take a box of old shoes as well.

Jack, I guess, said what all of us were thinking: "These people don't *deserve* Christmas!"

Perhaps he was right. But do any of us? How

[154

often, I wondered, did someone else do something nice that had gone unappreciated? How often did *we* turn out the light on Christmas? And so, with more charity in our hearts than we knew was there, we went home and sang to each other. There's always the possibility, of course, that we'd sounded awful.

SIX

The Philosophical Self

MINUTIA, INC.

I've had only one minor accident so far—I plowed into the back end of Ralph's car before we were married. This was not, of course, what endeared me to him. Twice, however, people have bumped into me while my car was standing still, and though their insurance covered the repairs, I was never compensated for the headaches.

I now have a new policy. Any time a dent amounts to less than a hundred dollars, I will say to the person at fault: "I will gladly pay the bill myself. You will compensate me by taking my car to three different garages to get the lowest possible estimate and bring them to me for my decision. You will then deal with the insurance company, make an appointment to have the repairs done, take my car in and arrange your own transportation home. You will make the necessary calls to determine when the car is ready, arrange transportation to the garage, check the work to see that it has been done properly, and bring my car back."

Ralph says he would pay a sizable amount just to

have the minutia of life taken care of. Perhaps some enterprising young person ought to start a service called Minutia, Inc. For a modest weekly charge, one could get trousers picked up at the cleaners, brakes checked, the lawnmower sharpened, the dog dewormed, and a new washer for the bathroom faucet. Or perhaps the service could stop at a home once a month to balance the checkbook, take shoes for repairs, clean out the refrigerator, carry newspapers to the dumpster, and sort through all the unmatched socks. Perhaps people could even subscribe for an annual visit just to get the aquarium cleaned, have the snow tires put on, or the kids taken for their inoculations.

I'm afraid, however, that such a service would spoil me beyond any hope of rehabilitation. I would start wanting Minutia, Inc., to take over the pulling on and off of children's boots, the cleaning of their ears, and the shopping for a ripe avocado.

But who knows? Perhaps it is the minutia of life that makes us appreciate the rest of living. If we'd never experienced the chore of scrubbing a roasting pan, could dinner at a restaurant ever taste so exquisite? And what could match the satisfaction of balancing a bank statement with twenty-seven checks outstanding and have it come out right the first time?

THE STATISTICIAN

Jack came home from school the other day completely incensed. He had homework in three subjects, he declared. He had to find a Confederate flag for a history skit. He had to call some dumb girl and tell her he'd taken her spelling paper by mistake. And he still hadn't sorted the laundry, his Saturday job. If he began working right now, he wailed, he wouldn't be through before 9:10, and would have only twenty minutes left before bedtime. Then he opened his mouth and bleated:

"It's not fair!"

I was about to agree that this was indeed an impressive list of chores for one night. I would resist telling him that his grandfather not only milked the cows every day when he got home from school, but chopped the wood as well. I would stifle the urge to tell him that if he just handled his time more efficiently, he'd be done by eight at the latest. I was, in fact, completely prepared to be sympathetic and supportive until he opened his mouth and bellowed out a P.S.:

"At least half of life is supposed to be play!"

Where, I wonder, is that writ? In what dusty law book, on what tablet of stone, is it engraved that no more than 50 percent of every day shall be work? What had we ever done to make Jack believe that anything over half would make him a dull boy?

He said he'd figured it out one morning when he woke up early and was waiting for me to make waffles. He said that not counting homework and household chores, most of what he did was work anyway: getting to sleep at night was work; getting up in the morning was work; eating asparagus was work; breathing was work; walking to school was work; waiting for waffles was work. There were, in short, several hundred varieties of work we had never even considered.

At this point I lost all objectivity, perspective, and humor. I told Jack that if waiting for waffles was such a chore, I could think of plenty of kids who might like to trade places with him. I told him that not only was it not writ anywhere at all that half of life was supposed to be play, but he might as well know that life was unfair as well. And I added that if he learned to cope with a little unfairness now, he'd be a lot better off in his later years.

Jack simmered down and peace was restored, but deep down I have this small nagging doubt: *Is* it supposed to be 50 percent, do you think, and did I miss something along the way?

BORROWING TROUBLE

The drawback to love is that the more people you care for, the more there are to worry about. I scarcely gave the idea of death a thought until I had my first baby and realized with sudden panic that the small helpless thing in my arms was dependent on me. I dared not die until she was twenty-one! Nothing must happen to Ralph! And what about the baby herself? Would she succumb to a mysterious crib disease? Where was that once-carefree me?

If I thought I had worries then, they were nothing compared to what I experienced after Jack and Peter came along. Three children meant three times the responsibility, the risk. Every moment of the day carried with it the possibility of broken arms and traffic accidents, brain tumors and leukemia. How would I keep my sanity?

In growing older, however, I've discovered that 90 percent of my worrying time is wasted, and that a lot of energy goes into fretting about "what if" situations that never get off the ground. Big worries. Medium worries. Little mundane worries.

I remember how I fussed when the grass wouldn't grow under a tree in the backyard. I spent several weeks agitating whether to try again or grow ivy, when the whole thing was resolved by a windy thunderstorm that blew the tree down.

Last month Susan was in a moral bind because she had accepted an invitation to go somewhere with somebody she didn't really care much about and later received a marvelous invitation for the same day from somebody else. What should she do? Which would this daughter of mine choose? How did I teach her that promises are important? The upshot was that when the big day arrived, Susan had the flu and couldn't go with either one.

And just this week Jack complained of thirst and weakness, and I panicked at the thought of diabetes. I had fed him too much sugar. It was all my fault. What would his life be like without a chocolate fudge birthday cake, and how would we all survive? It turned out that he was perfectly healthy, but while I'd directed all my anxiety onto him, Peter had developed an ear infection and was out of school for three days.

What was that line about having no thought for the morrow? Somebody read it to me again.

YOURS FOR THE ASKING

Ever since I noticed those ads in the miscellaneous sections of literary magazines, I've been curious. Not those ads stating that a sexually adventurous couple in their forties will consider anything, but those that advertise financial problems:

> Medical student needs money.
> Please send donations any
> amount. Box _____ N.Y.C.
>
> or
>
> Artist desires rich patron
> to continue her career.

I mean, we don't even get an explanation. Did the medical student squander his tuition at the race track? Is the artist in question working in oils, or does she draw cartoons for a P.T.A. newsletter? Are we to assume, on the basis of a half-inch ad, that people who are willing to publicize their plight are obviously worthy of our contributions and will use them to the best advantage?

Such ploys obviously work or people wouldn't

spend a dollar per word to put them in print. I might even compose one myself:

> Frazzled parents of three in
> urgent need of month-long trip
> to Bermuda. Box _____ Bethesda.

In fact, if a Catholic order can recruit men for the priesthood by advertising in *Playboy,* I wonder how much I could rake in if I stated simply:

> Curious woman wishes to know how
> much she would get by requesting
> that contributions be sent to her
> home in Bethesda.

ALBERT AND US

There are times when, despite a parent's best intentions, he comes off as an ogre of the first magnitude. The harder he tries to redeem himself, the worse he appears.

On a glorious Saturday in spring, Ralph stood at the dining-room window overlooking the backyard and remarked innocently that he really ought to cut down a small silver maple near the fence.

"Why?" asked Peter, Jack, and Susan in unison.

"Because it's scrawny," said Ralph.

"Would you have killed me if I had been born scrawny?" Peter wanted to know.

"Of course not," we exclaimed together. "That's different."

"A tree's alive, too," said Jack. "I don't see any difference."

"Listen. The silver maple is surrounded by bigger trees that block the sunlight. It's never going to get much bigger than it is now," Ralph told him.

"So?" chanted the kids.

"If I'd been born a midget, would you have cut my throat because I'd never get any bigger?" Susan questioned.

Ralph panicked. "But it will probably get diseased!"

"So kill us, too," Susan begged dramatically. "We may get diseased some day. Who knows?"

We decided to stop the discussion before it got any worse, and if Ralph had plans for the ax that day, he abandoned them.

But we're not out of the woods yet. We've had the same reaction with ants.

"Don't kill it!" Peter insisted as I started toward a large black ant crawling along the counter top. "Take it outside."

"If I take it outside, it will just come back in again," I told him. "Not only that, it will bring in all its cousins."

167]

"So doesn't it have a right to live? Hasn't it got a right to eat? What if it's a little kid and its mommy is waiting for it? How would you like it if I went on a trip and some big animal . . ."

We might as well throw out the fly swatter. I suppose we'll get the same thing when the wasps build their nest under the eaves again. Albert Schweitzer, come back. We need you. You can take our house for the summer, and we'll return around January 1 when everything alive is frozen solid, and we can postpone these moral decisions for another few months.

COMMON PHRASES

Peter declared recently that the worst words in the whole world were "Keep Out" or "Keep Off." Anywhere he ever wanted to go, he said, had a dumb sign on it.

Jack disagreed. "We are experiencing technical difficulties," he said, were the worst words he could think of.

But Susan, who loves to go barefoot, had her own ideas. "No shoes, no service," she said, were the most disagreeable words in the English language.

Kids! I thought as I was getting dinner later. *With wars and pestilence and pollution to worry about they get uptight over trivia such as that!* But the more I toyed with it, the more I realized that there were some phrases I, too, could do without. "While stirring constantly" was one. "Keeping yolks separate" was another. And what about "all six verses" or "no left turn"? What about "front end only" and "three times a day with meals"?

When dinner was over and Ralph and I lingered over our dessert I asked him if there were any phrases he could do without. He didn't even have to think about it. "Will you hold, please?" was one. "Salad extra," another, as well as "one way from four to six," "attach tab C to slot D," and "expires with this issue."

It's not the words, of course, that we hate so much. It's just the way they're arranged. It's all a matter of semantics, and it's nice to know that some phrases, such as "apply liberally" can refer not only to the palm of the hand on the seat of the pants, but to love and affection as well.

OF MATTHEW, MARK, AND CECIL B. DE MILLE

Like Paul's conversion, it was a long time in coming, but it looks as though it's going to stick. From prop man to producer, the people that walked in darkness have seen a great light and have undertaken to bring the Good Book to two-hundred million Americans.

It was a magnificent moment when Cecil B. De Mille took on the Ten Commandments. Solomon in all his glory would have choked at the cost, but Hollywood figured if the general public wouldn't go for the Ten Commandments, they wouldn't go for anything, and the movie was so popular that now it's having a revival. In between, there have been so many Biblical movies that you could hardly thumb through a movie guide without running into a Job or a Robe or a Judas.

Pick a man (David). Pick a woman (Bathsheba). Add five pagan princesses, six curvaceous concubines, and a bevy of bare-bellied dancing girls, and you bring the Word to half the adult population.

The changeover from secular to sacred is surprisingly simple. Long-haired heroes cash in their guitars

[170

for lutes. Barroom brawls become wine-cellar free-for-alls in which the strength of the leading character is as the strength of ten because his heart is pure. Levi's great-granddaughters lounge on couches tempting Moses and Aaron who are the sons of Amram who is the son of Kohath who is the son of Levi, which makes them all first cousins, but nobody cares.

It's really uncanny when you think about it—all this lust lying around for a thousand years not only uncopyrighted, but absolutely uncensorable. How am I supposed to tell Jack he can't see a rerun of *Samson and the Seven Miracles of the World?* ("He was temptation to a thousand and one women!" say the ads.) Susan came home from *Joseph and His Brethren* to announce that the hero *did* lie with his master's wife, which is not the way Genesis tells it. And when *Sodom and Gomorrah* came around again, even Peter was saving his pennies for a private peep into the emperor's orgies.

The possibilities, I'm afraid, are unlimited. "See the earth swallow Dathan and Abiram!" some future ad will say. "See the dogs eat Jezebel!" And what about a horror story called "The Headless Horseman of the Apocalypse?" I wouldn't be a bit surprised if someone took it into his head to film the Immaculate Conception.

If something isn't done about this soon, whole classes of children are going to troop to church on Sunday mornings and announce, "No, I haven't read the Book, but I've seen the movie."

FAME AND FORTUNE

Every so often you read a biography of a famous person and discover that when he was small, nobody recognized his genius. Teachers punished him, parents misunderstood him, and every time he tried to be creative, he was told he was being an obnoxious little kid. Somehow he survived and lived to tell the world how obtuse his environment had been.

I get to thinking about this every February. I wonder if George Washington was ever scolded for tramping through the house in muddy boots; or if Lincoln lost his allowance for smuggling a book under the covers. Did Ben Franklin spend an entire meal arranging peas around the rim of his dinner plate, and if he did, did his father say he would obviously never amount to anything?

I mean, how is a parent supposed to know? How are we supposed to tell if the kid who spends a glorious afternoon searching the sidewalk for pennies will grow up to be a bank president? And is the one who empties an entire box of Band-Aids in one day destined to be a doctor?

We don't know. That's the point. Maybe Picasso

once ruined his bedroom by smearing paint all over the walls. Maybe Heifetz once stepped on his father's violin and was walloped over the head with it. Maybe Faulkner or Steinbeck was sent to bed because he told such stories at the supper table.

I try to remind myself occasionally that what bothers me the most about my children may actually be genius in bloom. Besides, you can't be too careful. What if somebody writes a biography of them some day? What will they say about me? What if my children write an *autobiography,* for heaven's sake! Can you imagine what they could blab around?

MAGNIFICENT OBSESSIONS

Some people have to wash their hands seventeen times a day, some have to have chewing gum handy, some have to add up all the speed limit signs as they drive downtown, but my obsession is reading the newspaper. I mean, I *have* to read it. Not the want ads or the financial columns, but religiously, page by page, I have to go through the front section, the editorials, the book reviews, the entertainment guide, the people and places columns, the real estate . . . I'm hooked.

"Just throw them out," Ralph says to me as the papers accumulate by my stand, but I haven't the will power. There might be an article I could use for research, an announcement of a cancer preventative, suggestions for saving on your income tax, tips for repairing Venetian blinds, or the review of a play we were planning to see.

"If it's really important, you'll hear about it," Ralph says; but what if somebody forgets to tell me? What if I go to a party and everybody knows there was an earthquake in Pakistan except me? What if there's a postal strike or a bomb scare or a satellite dropping, and I don't know about it until it happens?

I found a solution when we took a two-week vacation in New England and decided to let a neighbor collect the papers instead of cancelling delivery. (Jack wanted the sports sections.) When we got home, along with shells from Rhode Island and sand from Maine and some lobster claws which Peter had salvaged along the way, I had a two-weeks' stack of newspapers to deal with.

I set aside an entire weekend to read them. I didn't care in what order they were read, and it just happened that the pile was upside down. I began with the most recent paper first.

It was then I discovered that by reading them all backwards, ending with the oldest, I could skip half of every article because I already knew how the story came out. I knew what Iran decided to do about its most recent crisis before I even knew what the crisis was. I could skip reviews of movies which were no longer playing, and, best of all, I read the correction for a chocolate soufflé before I came to the recipe itself, thus saving the whole family from a culinary disaster.

I'm not sure whether programming oneself backwards would solve all compulsions or not. If you dried your hands first, for example, before you washed them, would they remain wet for so long that you could cut down on the seventeen times a day? If you subtracted speed limit signs instead of adding the numbers, wouldn't you just stop when you got to zero and consequently cure yourself of your obsession?

Ralph says not to do anything rash. He says the American Psychological Association isn't ready for me yet, and I might want to study it a little further before I submit a paper.

LET'S HEAR IT FOR AUTUMN

Fall is far and away my favorite season. For a while, at least. Fall is dry beauty, not the soggy sumptuousness of spring blossoms. Fall hints of clear, crisp nights, not humid Washington summers.

Of course, you can get too much of a good thing. When the first leaves come down, I'm mad for a rake, relishing the crunch of dry foliage underfoot and reveling in the brilliance of its color. There is something infinitely satisfying in attacking a lawn cluttered with leaves and making it neat and tidy. Naturally the kids have to leap and run through the first big heap of the season, but we usually have the leaves bagged by twilight and often celebrate with the first fire of October.

By noon of the next day, however, the yard is covered again. At this point I hand the rakes to Susan, Jack, and Peter, and organize a race. By the third day I am paying so much per bag, and finally we reach a point where we stand at the window glaring up at the trees, speculating on how many more yardfuls are yet to fall.

But there's a purpose. November will come, when the ground is gray and the sky is gray and the whole world seems to have been painted flat. You will wonder if your soul itself is turning gray. Then you will remember that bare branches mean no more leaves, no more cluttered lawns, no more clogged rain gutters, no more heaps of rotting "gluk" waiting forlornly at the curb. If there were not so many leaves and so much work, we could not possibly find beauty in the month of November, I tell myself as I drag the sixteenth bag out to the street. And if the leaf disposal truck gets here before Christmas, I'd say the system was working well.

GRACIOUS LIVING

"Gracious" is a rather curious word. It's the exclamation my grandmother used whenever the cow got out of the pasture. It was a term my mother used to mean staying good-tempered and polite when subjected to rudeness.

These days, however, you hear a lot about gracious living. The real estate ads are full of it. It denotes a sort of quiet, comfortable luxury to which we all aspire.

I'm not so sure we'd all agree on what is a necessity and what's a luxury, however. To me, pheasant under glass, caviar, and cherries jubilee are ostentatious; so are square eggs and electric pencil sharpeners. There are others, however, to whom enough food to fill the stomach is a luxury; who could not conceive of people rich enough to order a meal in a restaurant and leave half of it on their plates.

Thorsten Veblen (*Theory of the Leisure Class*) would have a field day if he came back now. With the advent of the Concorde, people jet to New York for lunch and back to Paris again by evening. We have contests in stuffing our stomachs to see how many blueberry pies one person can consume.

Or consider this little announcement I read in the *Washington Post:* In Maryland there is a summer camp for dogs at a charge of fifty dollars per week. Like most summer camps, it has its requirements: the dog must be over six months old and "temperamentally suited to group activities." The animal has its program: an hour hike, an hour optional swim, a fifteen-minute private training session, and a brushing every day. It has carpeted, air-conditioned kennels, Muzak, and a choice of seven different menus. A camp bus comes around to pick up and deliver the dogs, and your pet will even bring home a report card at the end of his stay.

Those of us who can scarcely scrape together fifty dollars a week to send a child off to camp will view such arrangements as ostentatious living. Others regard them as mere comfort. It depends, I guess, on whether you walk on two legs or four, but I can imagine what Veblen would have to say about the Muzak.

IN DEFENSE OF THE
PURITAN ETHIC

Back in my salad days when I was brash and rebellious, I decided that the Puritan Ethic was practically Original Sin itself. It seemed utter idiocy that every activity worth doing must somehow be constructive or that every beautiful thing had to be deemed holy before it could be admired. According to the Puritan Ethic pleasure for pleasure's sake—no matter how harmless—was out, and work was the order of the day.

I'll admit I would still make a rather poor Puritan. I still have the heretical belief that every human being is entitled to a day now and then to be utterly slothful, to recharge his batteries without contributing much to polite conversation or the family welfare. I've had the audacity to tell my children that sex, in addition to being beautiful, is also fun. And laughter, in our family, is definitely in.

But gradually, over the years, idealism has given ground to practicality, and parenthood has turned me around 180 degrees. I find myself edging somewhat closer to the long-faced fathers of years ago—in spirit, anyway. I no longer feel it to be outrageous that one should get enjoyment from work. I think it's rather nice. In fact, I think it's imperative that if a person is to survive with his sanity intact, he should choose an occupation he will enjoy more than anything else and devote himself to it, be it preaching, teaching, or studying the chimpanzee.

Like the good women of colony times, I do not enjoy idleness. A husband and child can remain inert all day Saturday if they like, but somehow I believe that my own hands were predestined to stay busy. To watch TV for one hour without simultaneously doing something else seems a colossal waste of time. Have you any idea how little you have to look at the set to know what is going on?

And as for the ban on objects which have no practical value: I have just discarded, secretly, from my kitchen, an egg timer, a nutmeg dispenser, an orange slicer, and a scented pot holder—all given to me over the years by children with no appreciation of the Puritan Ethic.

PARCEL OF LOVE

Some friends of ours confided to us that their daughter, at twenty, is seeing a psychiatrist because she does not feel she was loved enough. The parents, who seem like warm, likeable people to me, are baffled and a little hurt.

Now, of course, I wasn't around during their daughter's childhood, so I can't say whether they were stingy with their affection or not. But it occurs to me that if everybody in the whole world who wishes he were given more love as a child would stand up, nobody would be sitting down.

I mean, how much is enough? When Peter sits on my lap he *never* wants to get off. He'd sit there from New Year's to Christmas if I'd let him. When Jack is stretched out in front of the fire and I'm giving him a good old-fashioned back rub, he never wants me to stop, though my fingers be worn to the bone. When Susan sits beside me on the couch to confide some of her problems, she would chatter away until five in the morning if nobody had to work the next day. *More,* their little egos seem to beg. *Forever and ever, more, more, more!*

I'm not so different myself. When Ralph has me in his arms, I never want him to go away. Each of us wants to be that protected fetus again, surrounded by softness and warmth and security.

I'm not sure just how I would react if Susan, Jack, and Peter were to go to a psychiatrist because they felt unloved. Maybe I'd go along, too, because that would make four of us; or perhaps I'd tell them to go with my blessing, and once they married and had children of their own, to please tell me how *they* managed to divide twenty-four hours between spouse, children, profession, and self, and still have enough hours left over to give each child that extra affection he craved.

They might end up realizing they got quite a bit of love and feel rather lucky, at that. If parents could put all their love in a package and tie it with ribbon, I'm sure it would be under every tree this Christmas. But love's not like that. It's like intravenous feeding: it's got to be continuous—slow and steady—and only a parent can possibly know how deep its source must be to keep it flowing twenty-four hours a day.

THE EASY LIFE

I wonder, sometimes, why it is that in addition to earthquakes and floods and all the things we can't control, we make life unnecessarily hard for ourselves. In addition to wars and other collective idiocies, we manage individually to make a mess of things, too.

If a person wants to let his own teeth decay, of course, that's his business. If he wants to overeat or paint his house every year or memorize long lists of useless information, so be it. But when he brings pain and suffering to others as well, there ought to be a law.

Why, for example, couldn't Beethoven have written everything in the key of C? Did he know how many people would fumble and sweat and weep at the piano over sonatas that had no business being sharped in the first place? Why couldn't *War and Peace* have been written in half the number of pages, and why couldn't Michelangelo have been assigned only the walls of the Sistine Chapel?

I was complaining about Beethoven to Ralph one

night, having flubbed a sonata for the third time. When I realized I had the attention of the children as well, I carried matters even further:

"Why can't kids get sick only in the daytime and never the middle of the night? Why can't they hate jelly sandwiches and love Brussels sprouts?"

The kids jumped in with both feet. They can tell the sublime from the ridiculous three miles away.

"Why can't snow stay around in the summer when we really need it?" Peter said.

"Why can't F's on report cards mean 'fabulous' and A's mean 'awful'?" said Jack.

"Why can't all mothers look like Farrah Fawcett-Majors?" asked Susan.

"Why can't Form 1040 be reduced to true or false instead of the sentence-completion type," said Ralph. "Why can't human beings reach their most attractive age and stay there the rest of their lives?"

We thought that last one over for a while. It would mean we'd never have had the pleasure of Gramp's stories, which have markedly improved since he reached seventy. Neither Ralph nor I could agree on what was the optimum age for either of us, and the kids had no intention of skipping their teens. We decided then and there that the only way to accept life was to accept change, the hard with the easy, the bitter with the sweet; so I kept my philosophical musings to myself and went back to butchering Beethoven.